The Old Pubs of
Gateshead

by John Boothroyd

Preface

This project started life as an exhibition held in 2008 for Gateshead Library's Local History Month. Research I carried out at that time has been used, but added to with some new material more suited to a book.

Much as we would all like to see it, a book of this size is not going to be all things to all people and I have had to put in some limitations. Please note!

Our 'Gateshead' is the old Parish and Borough of Gateshead: central Gateshead, Teams, Sheriff Hill, Wrekenton and Low Fell, but not Dunston, Whickham, Birtley or Felling.

The pages have been used for a survey of pubs, so an additional discussion of Temperance Bars, Clubs and Institutes has had to be excluded.

'Old Pubs' is being taken to mean those appearing in the Trade Directory survey on pages 44-47. This lists pubs advertising from 1889 up to 1939 (the last year in which Ward produced a full directory covering Gateshead). Those closing before 1889 and opening after 1939 are still discussed as part of a wider picture, but they take second place. There is a separate listing of post-war pubs on page 47.

Charabanc trip from the Queen's Head, Sheriff Hill around 1920.

I have used our 48 pages to provide a basic history of the pub scene in Gateshead over the years. You will not find here a rounded history of each pub, but I hope you will find that the occasional snippets provided are entertaining and informative. I have tried to include as many good historic photos as can be sensibly fitted in, as well as the data I have collected relating to older pubs.

It is impossible to estimate picture dates and write about pubs without being challenged on detail. I have put great efforts into being accurate, but all sources can at times prove unreliable. Please be positive; if you know any different and can back this up then do let me know on jbgatpubs@gmail.com and it may be possible to correct the text for any future reprint.

I hope you enjoy the book!

John Boothroyd, 2014

Previous page: Steamboat Inn and St Mary's Church around 1910.

Front cover: *Charabanc trip from the Alma Inn on Nuns Lane around 1920 (top).*
            Foresters' Arms on Derwentwater Road in 1961 (below).

Back cover: *Station Hotel on Hills Street in 1919 (top).*
            Foresters' Arms on Derwentwater Road in 1961 (below).

Copyright John Boothroyd 2014

First published in 2014 by

Summerhill Books PO Box 1210, Newcastle-upon-Tyne NE99 4AH

www.summerhillbooks.co.uk

email: summerhillbooks@yahoo.co.uk

ISBN: 978-1-906721-79-4

Part One
A Short History of Pubs in Gateshead

Gateshead's pub history is a little unusual for a British town: few pubs are of any great age, few pubs could be described as grand and most of those standing in 1945 have since been demolished.

Gateshead is a town that has traditionally lived in Newcastle's shadow. The grand buildings were on the north bank of the Tyne and Newcastle was (and is) the regional capital where most businesses and cultural institutions have chosen to locate themselves.

The presence of Newcastle might explain the lack of grand buildings; the huge changes in Gateshead's pub scene can be explained by the rapid growth in the town's population and the problems this left when growth petered out.

Population boomed in every decade from a mere 12,000 people in 1820 to a staggering 125,000 in 1920. This was Victorian Gateshead where new industries prospered, new residents were attracted from across Britain (and Ireland), but where 'prosperity' left a legacy of poor planning, poor building

Gateshead (Bridge Street) around 1920.

and a catalogue of social problems that the town's meagre public finances were incapable of solving.

Sadly for Gateshead the comparative good times reached a peak around 1900 and there followed a long period of decline. It would not be unfair to say that the wholesale demolition and redevelopment of the 20th century was driven by a determination to put these matters right and to embrace a modern and a better world.

Gateshead's old pubs are a reflection of a town built around heavy industry and commuting where the showpiece centre lay elsewhere. This was a town of packed terraces and yards, crowded and often insanitary to the north, still terraced but with more breathing space towards the centre and with some more spacious building on the southern fringe. The Gateshead of the old pubs was tough, was Spartan and was not pretty.

Early Gateshead, Early Inns

Nowadays the terms 'Public House', 'Inn', 'Tavern' and 'Hotel' are almost interchangeable. Back in time though, an **Inn** was an establishment for the accommodation, rest and refreshment of horse-borne travellers (including stabling for the horses) whilst a **Tavern** was more 'local'.

Public House began to be used from the late 1700s to describe places where activities and attractions also took place. The French word **Hotel** has been used since the early 1800s to describe a superior inn (for those who could afford it!)

Before 1820 three quarters of Gateshead people lived close to the river where the bridges now stand. Most of the remainder were sited along the South Shore riverbank or followed more southerly sections of the Great North Road though Sheriff Hill and the Wrekenton area.

The Cross Keys Inn on Pipewellgate around 1800.

Services Provided

Pubs have always provided accommodation and refreshment, especially for the traveller, a centre for local activities and a place for people to meet and relax. Over the years it has been the style, the mix and the competition that has changed rather than the basic services.

In the days before the railways, people moved around the country by horse and required a network of places to sleep (including stabling for their horses). Gateshead had a major coaching inn at the **Black Bull** and other High Street inns were used as starting points for more local journeys by carrier's cart. We can assume that the cluster of horse-related pub names at the foot of the High Street hark back to this trade (**Old Nag's Head, Coach and Horses, Grey Horse** and **Grey Nag's Head**).

We might wonder at the number of places calling themselves 'inn' or 'hotel' thereby implying accommodation, but Gateshead's inns, pubs and hotels also served as lodging houses for the many workers who were obliged to be mobile in order to find work.

Before the mid 1800s Gateshead had no

Bottle Bank, the Hawk (left) and the Full Moon (centre) around 1920.

sizeable meeting places other than its inns and this was true for both the middle and working classes. Almost all the clubs, societies and protest groups in the town would have formed in and met in those larger inns with meeting rooms.

A Trade Directory advert for the Queen's Head, 1863.

The Coach and Horses at Wrekenton around 1930.

In the days before local government offices, officials used rooms at the **Grey Horse** to hold inquests into accidents and at the **Goat**, magistrates held trials, churchwardens distributed charities and local freemasons held their lodge meetings.

Using a Low Fell example, the long room at the **New Cannon** was at the centre of village social activities hosting dinners, dances and society meetings (as well as travelling troupes of entertainers!)

Dispensary Balls at the **Grey Horse** might be the choice of some, but for the working classes the pub provided a centre for their own sports and social activities. Cock fights were common until banned in the mid 1800s and there were known pits at the **Black Bull** (High Street), the **Black Horse**, the **Three Tuns**, the **Travellers' Rest** and the **Ship** (at Wrekenton).

Gateshead's pubs were always far more than places to get drunk as many detractors claimed. Apart from places to socialize, they were also places for keeping informed about local employment opportunities and the hub of funeral, sickness and other benefit clubs.

Gateshead's Boom Years (from around 1830 to 1900)

In our early period the land close to Gateshead High Street was used for market gardening and the countryside started beyond West Street. In a very short space of time, the High Street became ribboned with terraces branching outwards. Bensham Road, what became Askew Road and Sunderland Road followed a similar pattern and new pubs were opened as part of the building development.

From about the 1840s the horse was gradually replaced by the railway as the main form of longer distance transport. New premises sprung up alongside stations such as the **Railway** (**Station**) on Hills Street.

In 1835 Gateshead became a Borough for the first time. Town Hall buildings were acquired or built and inns were not needed for local administration purposes.

Working Mens' Clubs began to pose a threat to the pubs in the final years of the 1800s. To attract and retain customers, landlords responded by promoting various forms of entertainment alongside the convivial drinking.

Concerts and musical entertainments (the informal 'free and easies') were popular, indeed the Musical Hall tradition evolved from pub beginnings. This was also an era in which many sports clubs grew from pub roots. Later on New Gateshead Football Club grew from the **New Gateshead Inn** and the Albert Blue Star FC from the **Albert**.

On a more genteel note membership of flower and horticultural societies based at pubs became a common Victorian pastime. Records from 1853 describe a full set of winners for the **Crown** Inn Flower and Vegetable show and the Team Colliery Horticultural Society show at the **Queen's Head** (which became the **Victoria**) – both in Low Fell.

Borough Arms outing around 1930.

Fun in Low Fell's 'Crown' around 1975.

The Masons' Arms and Chandless terraces around 1950.

Government Acts

During this period of growth, the Government tried all ways to counteract the effects of drink on local communities. Appalled by the effect of the gin houses, it relaxed the old licensing laws for selling beer. Gin was bad, beer was healthy (certainly compared to local water) and even the temperance movement supported their actions. For very little outlay the 'Beer House Act' of 1830 allowed 'beer-houses' to sell beer although a full licence for selling wines, spirits and beers was reserved for the 'public house' (short for 'public ale-house'). As licensing records show, 'beer-house' numbers were not very different from those for 'ale-houses'. They were small-scale enterprises, often just a room in a house and served a clientele from nearby streets.

The Steamboat and Tyne Bridge around 1925.

The 1830 Beer House Act did not work as the Government had hoped and the 1869 Wine and Beer House Act tried to put the lid back on by giving magistrates powers to refuse the granting or renewing of licences. The decline in the number of pubs began as long ago as this. As it has proceeded steadily ever since, it cannot be taken as the 'recent' phenomenon so often claimed.

Hard Times in Gateshead (the period from about 1900)

Despite these tougher times, the pubs and beer-houses still remained a core part of local community life. However attitudes in society were changing and pubs continued to lose ground in competition for leisure time with theatres then cinemas, then wireless, then television. Indoor sports were introduced. Quoits pitches and sheds appeared shortly after 1900 but died a death within 30 years (the **Patent Hammer**, the **Fountain**, the **Plough** (on Old Durham Road) are all known to have been quoits-playing pubs). Pubs with room to do so introduced billiards but were eventually overtaken by the purpose-built billiard halls. They did score successes though: the popular charabanc outings allowed locals an escape for a while during the hard years between the wars and, as the pictures on the front cover and pages 2 and 5 show, these were often based around the local pub.

The 1869 Act was followed by an Act in 1904 which allowed pubs to be closed (with compensation) if deemed 'redundant' or 'badly adapted'. Both Acts concentrated owners'

New High Street roundabout and Rowell's bottling works in 1959.

The Waggon Team around 1950.

The Old Fold Tavern around 1965.

minds into upgrading their most viable pubs. In the early years of the century many were upgraded or rebuilt at the same location (for example the **Brown Jug, Cross House**, the **Honeysuckle**, the **Magpie**, the **Three Tuns** and the **Seven Stars**). Beer-houses were abolished in the 1950s having been given the choice of folding or upgrading to full license, although many had already done so in the preceding years.

Many older pubs were lost but the closure not challenged as owner attention had moved to building new pubs on the out-of-town housing developments and old licences were simply transferred. All parties knew a 'shakeout' was inevitable and a picture emerges of the forces concerned with law and order, with morality and with business interests jockeying to achieve an acceptable new balance.

Radical housing and transport plans had been drawn up for the town. New pubs close to new estates included the **Jolly Miller** (Chowdene), the **Wrekendike** (Springwell estate, Wrekenton) and the **Three Feathers** (Lyndhurst estate, Low Fell). The place of the car and the pub in the thinking of owners can be seen in the location and layout of the 'neo-Georgian' style **Waggon Team** at Lobley Hill.

Roads were widened, roundabouts and bypasses created and in central Gateshead alone dozens of old pubs were lost at both ends of the High Street (roundabouts), to the east (bypass) and on what remained of the High Street (to road widening for better access).

Demolition of the worst housing and a programme of rebuilding began a process that continued on a grand scale until the 1970s. The central riverside area was cleared between the wars and after the last war so were the neighbourhoods along the High Street, West Street, Bensham Road, Askew Road and Sunderland Road. More old pubs died.

The Present and Future

The new pubs have joined the remaining 'Old Pubs of Gateshead' into the modern era. But this is not a happy period for the local pub. The pub is still a place to chat and unwind, a place to celebrate (and commiserate) life's occasions. But society has changed radically, the world is a very different place from even 30 years ago and publicans compete in a crowded marketplace for the business of the modern consumer.

How many Gateshead pubs can survive, what tactics they will be using to keep and win business, where the successful players will be found are all unknowns. Businesses have always needed to adapt, but this current era is one that genuinely threatens a long-established institution at the heart of communities. What will a book on pubs have to say in 20 years time? How far will it be 'Time Gentleman, please' for the 'Old Pubs of Gateshead'?

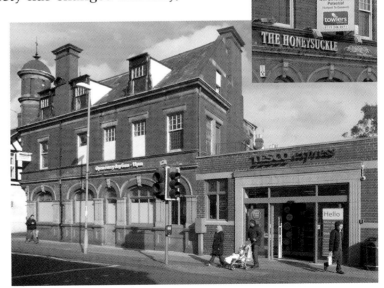

The Honeysuckle in 2008 (inset) and 2014.

Part Two
A Tour of the Town
Gateshead's Riverside

The riverside area was Gateshead's earliest centre: an historic hub at the south end of the Tyne Bridge. The 'Great North Road' ran south to London and north to Edinburgh and provided the best commercial locations on Bridge Street, Bottle Bank and up onto the High Street. Gateshead's most important inns were all here or were close by. Even by the early 1800s Gateshead was expanding out from this cramped hillside and later bridges made the area's main inns irrelevant.

The High Level Bridge (1849) was the first to divert through traffic, followed in 1928 by the New Tyne Bridge which took further traffic and pub buildings as well.

The riverside and the pubs it supported declined and most had gone by the Second World War. Period photographs show old inns in not-so-splendid isolation such as the **Full Moon** on Bridge Street and the **Steamboat** on Church Street (p6).

To the east of the Great North Road below St Mary's Church lies Hillgate, with the iron works of Hawks, Crawshay and John Abbot and Co beyond. The railings of St Mary's Church can be seen in our picture of the former **Robin Hood Inn**.

The former New Bridge Inn around 1930.

The Full Moon around 1930.

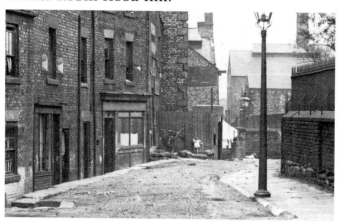
The former Robin Hood around 1920.

The Crown and Thistle around 1910.

Many of the district's buildings were old and at one time some would have been grand. The former Rectory building later housed the **Brandling Arms** and the former Town Hall on Oakwellgate the **Bush Inn**. As industrialisation progressed, the original inhabitants moved to the outskirts of town leaving their homes to be sub-tenanted for the poorer classes.

To the west of the bridge lies Pipewellgate, formerly a dark, dirty and cramped mix of housing and toxic industry; the picture taken outside the **Crown and Thistle** describes life down Pipewellgate better than any words can do.

Just along Pipewellgate was the **Fountain**, managed by Isaac Tucker before he moved up the bank to brew beer at the Turk's Head. It is said to be the oldest inn in Gateshead, although was rebuilt on several occasions. The building in the picture was the last rebuild (about 1905) and the last traditional inn open in Pipewellgate. It was later used by a Rowing Club and still stands today.

The **Globe Inn** in our picture was further down Pipewellgate and nearer to the King Edward Bridge.

Outside stands William Lockie originally an iron ship riveter from Wallsend who was licensee from 1911 until the 1920s and later steward of the British Legion Club.

The Fountain Inn around 1925.

Right: Landlord William Lockie outside the Globe around 1912.

Climbing up from the river we would have come to the **Goat** on Bottle Bank also described in the introduction and on page 40. In 1925 the **Goat** was on the wrong side of Bottle Bank to avoid the new Tyne Bridge. Although demolished, its legacy lives on as the carved goat that adorned its frontage was rescued and now lives happily in the Shipley Art Gallery.

Gateshead's coaching inn, the **Black Bull**, would also have been in the line of Tyne Bridge construction but had ceased trading by this time. It had boasted 20 living rooms and accommodation for over 100 horses, but had outlived its purpose and the site had been taken over by Snowball's Department Store.

On the safe side of the road (well safe for a further 80 years) was the **Queen's Head Hotel**, the riverside's last surviving traditional pub. The history of the **Queen's Head** illustrates well the great variety of social activities and services that the old inns could provide and why they were so central to community life.

The Goat in 1921.

At different times, the rooms of the **Queen's Head** were the temporary Town Hall (1867), a courthouse, a temporary home for the Roman Catholic Mission (when the Catholic chapel was destroyed in the Hillgate fire of 1854), a billiard room and a 'Harmony Hall' (Variety Theatre). In the days of stagecoaches, the **Queen's Head** was also a busy post-house. It served drinks as well!

Left: The Queen's Head by the Tyne Bridge in 2000.

Around the Stations

The **Half Moon Inn** was traditionally one of Gateshead's finest and earliest and a great rival to the nearby **Queen's Head**. It was rebuilt and reopened in 1891 with a curve rather than a corner after a tram became derailed and crashed into its structure. With rooms, a restaurant, small and large dining rooms, bars, a billiard room, a smoke room and a lounge, it claimed to be the up market facility Gateshead had been waiting for and was renamed the **Half Moon Hotel**. There were a number of bars: a small 'High Bar' further along Half Moon Lane survived into the 21st century and the one on the curve featured in the Billie Whitelaw film 'Payroll'.

The Half Moon Hotel around 1930.

Wine and spirit merchants Davison and Wood Ltd ran the premises for most of its lifetime and for a period in the 1980s it was 'Wheeler's' night club. It was controversially demolished to make way for development that included the Hilton Hotel.

The **Central's** building was constructed in 1854 for wine and spirit merchant Alderman Potts before becoming a hotel in the 1890s. The pub underwent a £1.5m grant-aided refurbishment in 2009 and is regarded as one of Britain's 'Real Ale Heritage Pubs'. In the film adaptation of 'Women in Love', Glenda Jackson found herself propositioned here but was 'rescued' by Oliver Reed.

The unassuming **Station Hotel** (back cover) has quietly 'watched' whilst its grander neighbours on Half Moon Lane

The Central Hotel building around 1850.

have gone through their various upheavals and film set moments. It has served time as a more traditional pub but also as a 'Real Ale' bar and can trace its roots back to the old **Railway** mentioned in Trade Directories in the 1850s.

Above: The Half Moon Hotel (High Bar) in 1983.

Right: The Commercial Hotel in 1966.

Along Gateshead's High Street

Gateshead's old High Street was a great talking point for previous generations on two counts: its long length and the number of pubs it supported.

Before it was redeveloped, Gateshead indeed boasted the longest High Street in England from Bottle Bank to the Old Durham Road and if plotted by pubs ran in continuous length from the (bottom) **William IV** at no. 10 to the **Argyle** at no. 423.

The number of pubs and beer-houses was of course forever changing but topped 30 and varied from humble mid-terrace establishments such as the **Golden Fleece** to ornate hotels such as the **Metropole**.

South of the railway line lay a cluster of pubs which disappeared as the rail bridge was widened and the new roundabout built in 1959.

The **Old Nag's Head** at no. 59 was managed by 'Tot' Anderson's family (see also p43). It was popularly known as 'Tot's Totally Free House' with a reputation for supplying '*free cheese and biscuits, pickled onions and on occasions, tripe and trotters to those with less in their pockets than most*'. The picture shows 'Tot' junior and family outside their pub. The dog was called 'Monty' and had a liking for whisky and beer. He was also fond of tram rides and the family was frequently called out to retrieve their drunken dog when he boarded trams other than those on his usual route.

Next along at no. 65 was the **Dun Cow** (originally the **Red Cow**), which had only just been rebuilt from its old 17th century premises (p40). Great play was made of transferring its ornate period ceiling to the first rebuild, but no press mention has been found about the special ceiling when it was obliged to move again. This last **Dun Cow** building still exists although with traffic and no surrounding housing it died as a pub in the 1970s.

Bottom of the High Street around 1959. Coach and Horses and Turk's Head (left), Dun Cow and Old Nag's Head (right).

The Old Nag's Head with Tot Anderson Jnr and family around 1950.

The **Grey Horse** at no. 99 was at one time the largest hotel in town and has already been mentioned in our introduction as the location for many important public gatherings. After demolition, its name did re-emerge for a newly built pub on the Chandless estate before that was later re-christened the **Lindisfarne**.

On the west side of the road the **Turk's Head** at no. 66 was part of Tucker's Brewery (called the 'Turk's Head Brewery' – see page 41). After it ceased to trade as a pub in the 1950s the premises were used by Working Mens' Clubs.

BALL
GIVEN BY
JOSEPH ROBSON, ESQ.,
MAYOR OF GATESHEAD,
IN THE
GREY HORSE INN LONG ROOM,
GATESHEAD,
ON THE
23RD, OCTOBER, 1851.
CONDUCTOR OF THE ORCHESTRA,
MR. M. LIDDELL.

Above: Grey Horse Ball programme, 1851.

Left: The Grey Horse around 1950.

The **Coach and Horses** at no. 76 was the last old pub in the area, but this closed in 1971 when the new road was developed through the former brewery district between High Street and West Street.

The start of the 'new' High Street was now where the **Crown Hotel** (no. 137) and Rowell's 'New Brewery' stood (p42), but neither of these businesses weathered the changes. As can be seen from the photograph (best shown on page 42) theirs was an impressive frontage in marble at ground level and with elegant classical architecture above. The site built over an earlier much humbler **Crown** as well as the **Lord Raglan** beer-house. From the **Crown** we would have passed the tiny **Ship** at no. 169 before finally coming to the **Grey Nag's Head** at no. 219, now our first surviving High Street pub and once known as the 'Top Nag's' as opposed to the 'Bottom Nag's' which was Tot's place.

Crossing the road from the **Crown** we could have called in for a swift 'gill' at the **Albion** (no. 148), the **Ellison Arms** (no. 164) (see p39), at the **British Queen** (no. 176), the **Waggon** (no. 214) and the **Atlas** (no. 244) before we reached our next 'survivor' – the **Metropole**.

The Coach and Horses and Tucker's Brewery in 1965.

The Albion in 1964.

The British Queen around 1935.

The Albion (left), new Dun Cow (centre), Rowell's Brewery and the Crown Hotel (right) in 1964.

The two women in the photograph of the **British Queen** were sisters Lily and Emily, daughters of landlord Percy Anderson whose name appears on the sign above. Percy was brother to 'Tot' senior whose family we met at the **Old Nag's Head**.

He is remembered by granddaughter Joyce Robson as being immaculately and formally dressed with pin-striped trousers, white apron, starched collar and beautifully polished shoes. This would have been the norm for landlords whose task was to set a good example and maintain order. When the **British Queen** closed, its licence was transferred to the **British Queen** on Split Crow Road.

The Grey Nag's Head around 1970.

The Ship in 1965.

The **Metropole Hotel** (no. 246) was built around the Metropole Theatre, opened in 1896 and as such is probably Gateshead's grandest pub building. It retains some of its original features inside but in common with most pubs now has one open space rather than separate rooms. On the top floor is a room formerly used for concerts and entertainment and on the first floor the remains of an elegant, spacious function room and bar. There are fond memories from the 1970s when former High Street residents returned in droves from the outskirt estates for their New Year's Eve celebrations at the 'Met'.

Robert Drummond outside the Waggon around 1900.

The Metropole before Charles Street widening in the 1960s.

More pubs survived at the southern end of the High Street than at the north. On the terraced east side of the High Street there was a shakeout of the smaller establishments: the **Butchers' Arms** (no. 257), the **Rector House** (no. 293), the **Golden Fleece** (no. 309) (p34) and the **Peareth Arms** (no. 337) all disappeared in time although only with the **Butchers' Arms** was this with forced re-development. The buildings of the **Rector House** and the **Golden Fleece** still stand though their drinking days are long gone.

Some of the land in this area was owned by the Peareth family and would have been the reason why the beer-house was so named. It was better known however as the 'Weighbag' (the spelling varies) and a look at the 1851 Ordnance Survey map of the area shows a Weigh House on this site.

Surviving on the east-side terrace is the **Old Fleece** which joined more substantially built pubs such as the **Phoenix**, the **William IV**, the **British Lion** and the **Blue Bell** into the modern era. With two 'Fleeces' in the same area the **Old Fleece** was also the 'Big Fleece' whereas the **Golden Fleece** was unsurprisingly known as the 'Little Fleece'. When the **Golden Fleece** finally closed its doors, its full licence was transferred to the new **Old Fold Tavern** (p7).

The **Phoenix** (p39 – now better known as 'Curley's') was run for 50 years by Mr Will Curley who was a world champion boxer. Curley was related to the Andersons (see pages 11, 12 and 43), had Irish roots and did extra

The Atlas around 1920.

The Park House Hotel during demolition in the 1960s.

business by attracting in others with an Irish background. His real name was Cawley, but at his win, the press misheard his Gateshead accent and publicised him as 'Curley'. The name stuck. The pub was also run by son Robert, who sold it to Scottish and Newcastle Breweries in 1964. The **Phoenix** was one of several larger pubs in the immediate area that made use of rooms above the main pub for functions including music and family events. This was also the case for the **William IV** and the **Blue Bell** across the road.

The Old Fleece around 1960.

The Rector House around 1960.

The nearby **British Lion** only closed for business within the last few years having traded since 1986 as the **Moon and Sixpence**. In a letter to the Gateshead Post in 1981, a Mrs Routledge describes a more traditional pub run by her father with spittoons and sawdust on the floor and a stuffed pony in a glass case 'which brought in lots of customers to see it'. Curiosity 'conversation piece' decor such as this went in and out of favour as clean lines, open and uncluttered spaces became more favoured between the 1920s and 1970s.

The William IV around 1910.

Wider road access to the High Street was responsible for the demise of the **Park House Hotel** (no. 253), the **Atlas** (no. 244) and the **Butchers' Arms** (no. 257), but at the southern end the long street that originally ran seamlessly into the Old Durham Road was cut short by a roundabout linking the new A1 viaduct (as it was originally called) and the Durham Road. The **Argyle** (no. 423) and the **Brunswick** (no. 27 Old Durham Road) were both lost.

The British Lion around 1925.

The Blue Bell (left) around 1960.

A trawl of the Trade Directory and licensing records show several of these old pubs had links with even older establishments. It isn't always clear whether a name change signified a new owner or just new branding, but trading earlier on the **Blue Bell** site was the **Brewers' Arms**, at the **Phoenix/Curley's** was the wonderfully named **Gorilla, Hercules** was there before the **Waggon** and there was a **Highlander** living at the **Atlas**. In days gone by, names often moved around with owners and the **Waggon** was trading at no. 194 whilst **Hercules** was occupying no. 216. By 1874 the **Waggon** had moved to nos. 214-216 where it stayed. Plotting people and pubs is rarely a straightforward business!

The Argyle (right) around 1960.

East of the High Street
Oakwellgate (south), East Street and the Chandless District

A brief look at the map on page 24 will show that building in the northern part of central Gateshead looks different from the terraces of the south and west.

The Flying Horse around 1920.

The Barley Mow and the Crawshay in 1963.

This was the area of yards and chares, a hotch-potch of early unplanned building that mixed industry and housing in the same area. Some of it had been comparatively grand but later degenerated into little more than overcrowded slums. In comparison to the yards the grid terraces further south were positively palatial!

Oakwellgate was an early Gateshead district straddling both sides of the railway viaduct. The **Flying Horse** (pictured) and the **Crystal Palace** (p40) were the more substantial pubs in the district.

Two pubs in our area closed and were taken over by Working Mens' Clubs. At no. 14 East Street stood the **Plough** whose premises were taken over by the Gateshead Disabled and Ex-Servicemen's Club and Institute. The Imperial Club (later the Gateshead Central Social Club) took over the former **Swan** further south on Swan Street.

East Street ran south from Oakwellgate and parallel with the High Street. Four pubs here suggest two important themes: the **Barley Mow** at no. 28 and the **Plough** remind us that until the great expansion of the town in Victorian times, that this was the market gardening area that fed the town to the north. The **Crawshay** at no. 22 and the **Hawks' Arms** at no. 50 remind us that Hawks, Crawshay were one of the great iron making firms of the town and would have employed many of the residents nearby.

BOROUGH
OF
GATESHEAD.

Notice is hereby given, that the Police of this Borough have Instructions to preserve good Order, particularly on Sundays, in the PUBLIC HOUSES and BEER HOUSES in the Borough; and to Summon before the Magistrates every Publican and Beer House Keeper who shall encourage or permit Disorder in his House.

Persons who may suffer Depredations, are requested to give the EARLIEST POSSIBLE NOTICE thereof, to Mr. Usher the Superintendent of the Police, at the Police Offices in Oakwellgate, for facilitating the Discovery and Apprehension of Depredators, and the Recovery of stolen Property.

By Order of the Watch Committee.
William Kell,
TOWN CLERK.

Gateshead, 19th April, 1836.

STEPHENSON, PRINTER, BRIDGE STREET, GATESHEAD.

Above: The Richard Cobden in 1960.

Left: Public disorder in pubs! – Gateshead Corporation warning dated 1836.

Those critical of pubs in the past made many valid arguments connected with drunkenness, domestic violence and the effect on family income of reckless drinking, but at times these arguments were too one-sided. Many Gateshead trades demanded liquid intake and beer was safer than the insanitary local water supply. Miners and chemical workers needed to clear away dust, whilst workers in the iron and glassmaking trades needed to rehydrate after working in stiflingly hot conditions.

The **Crawshay** was favoured by workers from John Abbot and Co before the latter closed in 1909. Sowerby's Ellison glassworks and metalworking firms such as Armstrong Whitworth kept most of the East Street pubs in business. Tales are told of lads from these pubs carrying billy cans of beer marked with workers' names and suspended on long poles to quench the

The Ellison Arms on Park Lane in 1963.

thirst of those working on the other side of the street. Now that must have been a sight!

The Chandless district at the south end of East Street was built in the 1850s and 1860s. Typical of this area are the pubs that could be found on many street corners and these would have been supplemented by a number of beer-houses usually mid-terrace properties.

Most pubs in this area seemed to have had nicknames. The **Prince of Wales** was 'Lumsden's' (after Bob Lumsden the landlord), The **Hawks' Arms** was 'Black Tom's' (probably after Thomas Hunter, landlord in the 1880s) and the **Ellison Arms** here was better known as the 'Red Bar' to distinguish it from the **Ellison Arms** on the High Street. The **Black Swan** took the name the 'Mucky Duck' or sometimes the 'Dirty Duck', also used by the **White Swan** on Windy Nook Road but with far less justification! On the edge of this district stood the **Shipcote Hotel** named after the colliery which operated on the opposite side of the road until the 1880s (now the bus depot site). The **Shipcote** is remembered as a pub with a great domino playing tradition. The pub sign indicated ownership by Chipchase and Co, hence another nickname – 'Chippies'.

The Black Swan around 1955.

The Shipcote around 1910.

West of the High Street
Along West Street and Prince Consort Road

The Lord Nelson around 1970.

The Princess of Wales in 1971.

The Black Bull on Mulgrave Terrace around 1910.

The High Street was most definitely Gateshead's drinking Mecca. Although of a sizeable length itself, Gateshead's West Street (running into High West Street) boasted noticeably fewer pubs and beer-houses.

Away from the West Street we could find our familiar pattern of grid terracing supported by a network of corner street pubs.

To the north of our district was the **Lord Nelson**, where on the wall the upper torso of a partly clad lady greeted pub users. (This was presumably an attempt to replicate the figurehead of a ship in Nelson's navy!)

The **Clavering Arms** (p36) and **Eagle** (both on Mulgrave Terrace) were demolished as part of the Barn Close slum clearance programme in the 1930s. The nearby **Princess of Wales** was rebuilt '*at the corner of … a proposed new road from Askew Road to West Street*' (Archive records), marooned as in the picture for several years before also being demolished. Older residents knew it as 'the Irish Bar' and it was patronised by the large numbers of people in central Gateshead with Irish roots.

The third and oldest pub on Mulgrave Terrace – the **Black Bull** – still survives, though somewhat cut off from central Gateshead by the modern link road.

The **Talbot Hotel** stood close to the site of the recently demolished **Trafalgar**. Curious snippets sometimes get written up in the local press and the **Talbot's** landlady Mrs Snowdon generated some interest by running extra business from her hotel where you could also order your coffin!

Further down West Street, on the Jackson Street corner, stood the elegant **Old Mill** whose licence was transferred to the new **Springfield Hotel** at the end of the 1930s. Further back in history there was indeed an old mill on this site and this was one of several Gateshead pubs named after the town's windmills (see p40).

The Talbot in 1961.

The Prince Consort in 1968.

The Neville Hotel in 1966.

The **Star** (p35) and the **Neville** were the more important establishments along High West Street. The **Neville** is remembered as a popular drinking place for workers from Jackson the Tailors' factory a few streets further south.

The area between West Street and Prince Consort Road that currently houses the Civic Centre and St Joseph's RC Primary School was terraced until the 1960s with a large set of corner street pubs. Presumably because they were all on or just off Prince Consort Road, most were honoured with regal names. These included the **Albert**, the **Prince Alfred**, the **Prince Consort** and further west the **Prince of Wales** – a sure case of patriotism combined with quality branding!

Top of the local tree was the **Royal Hotel** (p35), an imposing stone built premises located on Prince Consort Road (west side) opposite the present-day Primary School. Matthew Swinburne of Swinburne and Co was the original manager here. At the other end of the size scale was the **Albert** (known locally as the 'Little Albert' to distinguish it from the **Prince Albert** and the **Royal Albert** elsewhere in town). It was thought to be the smallest pub in Gateshead, though as might be expected, this was always a matter of pub debate.

The Albert around 1960 – 'The Little Albert'.

The Prince Alfred around 1960.

Of the old pubs only the **Black Bull** remained west of the High Street after the clearance work had been completed. In time this was joined by the **Gloucester** (a rebuild of an earlier beer-house located slightly further north). This was one of the few old pubs rebuilt in central Gateshead: the **Dun Cow** on the High Street was one, as was the **Barley Mow** on East Street. The link between the old **Grey Horse** and the new on the Chandless estate is there but not quite as strong. Of these, only the **Gloucester** remains in business. The new **Barley Mow** and **Grey Horse** have been demolished. As noted elsewhere, the **Dun Cow's** second rebuild has long since ceased to trade as a pub.

The Wylam (Wylam and Hector Streets) in 1963.

The Bee Hive (Prince Consort Road and Arthur Street) about 1920.

West Gateshead
Along Bensham, Askew and Coatsworth Roads

Along with much of Windmill Hills, the **Borough Arms** on Bensham Road was traditionally owned by the 'Borough Holders of Gateshead' who from medieval times held land and property rights in exchange for helping administer the town. It has always had the look of a country pub and before the great expansion of the town to the west indeed it was. Bensham Road and Derwentwater Road were the old roads out to Hexham and the Teams, but Askew Road cut through the old Redheugh estate of the Askew family.

The Borough Arms around 1920.

Terraces sprouted from all these roads insofar as geography and rail lines would allow. The area became particularly popular after the first Redheugh Bridge was opened in 1871, when homes here became convenient not only for the Greenesfield railway works but also for the Armstrong works in Elswick.

The **Askew Arms** was built as part of the Askew Road terracing with alterations in 1909. Still small in comparison to the nearby **Redheugh Hotel**, it is remembered as sporting a stuffed dog behind the bar (a 'champion ratter' Jack Russell!). Beyond the **Redheugh Hotel** was Askew Road West on which stood the **Beaconsfield Hotel**, an 'Irish' pub better known as 'Donny's'.

The Askew Arms around 1960.

Derwentwater Road leads down from St Cuthbert's Church and Bensham Road. On the way down you would pass **Glasgow House** (the 'White House') before reaching a local landmark at the junction with Askew Road West. This was the **Foresters' Arms** (front and back cover) known to all as the 'Coffin'. Several old inns in the town were substantially rebuilt shortly after 1900 and invariably rebranded 'hotels'. The nearby **Magpie** (p40) was one of these – a pub well supported by workmen from Redheugh Iron and Steel, Davidson's glassworks and other Low Teams firms. The last pub in Gateshead was the **Lord Eslington Arms**, just beyond the River Team and better known as 'the Ezzy'. Of all Gateshead's districts this has been the most redeveloped. Nothing remains of any traditional pub, although the **Foresters' Arms** was rebuilt only to be closed within the last decade.

The Redheugh in 1966.

The Beaconsfield around 1960.

The Magpie in 1974.

By modern standards, Bensham is densely populated, but would have been spacious in comparison with the High Street. The further away from the river, the higher the standard of terracing built. This may account for fewer pubs – such establishments were often discouraged in the more select neighbourhoods and after 1869 magistrates had more powers to turn down applications. Covenants on some lands sold for housing also prohibited the building of pubs, which is one reason why the Bensham and Saltwell district is such a pub-free zone.

Within this area though is the **Azure Blue** on Eastbourne Avenue. This was previously the Co-operative Stores' local off-licence until it was allowed to become a pub. An 'Azure Blue' is a type of butterfly, but this was supposedly the second choice for a name of the new pub after locals objected to it being called the 'Painted Lady' – or so the story goes!

Sadly, the **Azure Blue** hit national headlines in 1994 with the murder of landlord George Gill. A colourful character, better known as Vivian, he had previously been landlord of the **Crown** on Coatsworth Road.

The **Springfield Hotel** also had a 'non-residents' bar separate from the hotel with an entrance opposite the fire station. From the 1930s it was well used by people from the (pub-free) Avenues district and students from the 'Tech' looking for a pie and a pint at lunchtime. The **Springfield Bar** vanished in the 1970s when the hotel was renovated.

Moving down Bensham Road, the **Castle** and the **Five Wand Mill** were both housed in substantial and well-constructed buildings. The **Five Wand Mill** was one of the larger pubs in the area with several rooms downstairs and a large function room upstairs. It survived into the 21st century before its site was redeveloped for housing, a fate also suffered 40 years previously by the tiny **Burton House** just a few streets further up. Further down Bensham Road the **Ravensworth Hotel** (originally the **Ravensworth Castle**) has been renamed again as the **Bensham Jockey** reflecting the fact that many local streets are named after racecourses. For

The Castle around 1965.

The Five Wand Mill around 1980.

years it was known as 'Joicey's' – John and later Isabella Joicey were long-time licensees up until the 1920s.

At the junction of Rawling and Bensham Roads two pubs stood on opposite corners. Occupying the site currently housing a Medical Practice was the **Gardeners' Arms** run by three generations of the Simm family and known as either 'Old Nick Simm's' or 'Simmies'. On the south side and still trading is the **Whickham House** (aka the 'Wicked Hoose' and sometimes 'Peggy's').

Many of the streets around Saltwell Road were built by John Ross who also built **Stirling House** for his own use. The drinking establishment **'Stirling House'** traded as a beer-house until 1938 when it upgraded and took over the full licence from the **Full Moon** on Bridge Street (p8). Known for a while as the **Tynesider**, it has been a popular venue for live music and later discos but along with others with the space for such activities such as the **Globe** (Old Durham Road) the **Travellers' Rest**, the **(White) Swan**, and the **Honeysuckle** found this could bring problems in a residential area (witness the columns of the Gateshead Post!)

A continuation of Bensham Road leads us to Lobley Hill. Gateshead has been enlarged on several occasions and between the wars took in land on both sides of the River Team including Lobley Hill. The **Lord Eslington Arms** (discussed on page 21) became a Gateshead pub. The new **Waggon Team** (p7) was built within the new Borough boundaries.

The Ravensworth in 1979.

The Gardeners' Arms in 1963.

Coatsworth Road supported three pubs, although the **Crown** (p35) at the junction of Bensham Road is the only one currently trading. Behind the **Crown** stood the **Victoria**, invariably called 'Dan Kane's' or 'Danny's' even though Dan Kane was landlord in the 1880s. Just off Coatsworth Road was the **Prince of Wales** (Hampden Street) better known as the 'Hen and Chicks' probably after the shaping of the Prince of Wales feathers.

Terraces off Coatsworth housed many of the skilled workers from the Greenesfield railway works. They were better built than those off Askew Road and the architecture of the **Honeysuckle Hotel** (p7) with its marble front and domed tower reflects a more affluent neighbourhood. Its history is similar to the **Magpie**: an old 'inn' rebranded 'hotel' after a substantial rebuild around 1900. It was considered one of the most profitable in the town, had several rooms including a 'Gentleman's Bar' and a spacious function room upstairs but suffered as a result of a number of neighbourhood problems and was closed as a pub. Although damaged in an arson attack (2008) it reopened in 2013 as a 'Tesco Extra' shop.

The Whickham House in 1984.

The Victoria and the Crown on Coatsworth Road in the late 1960s.

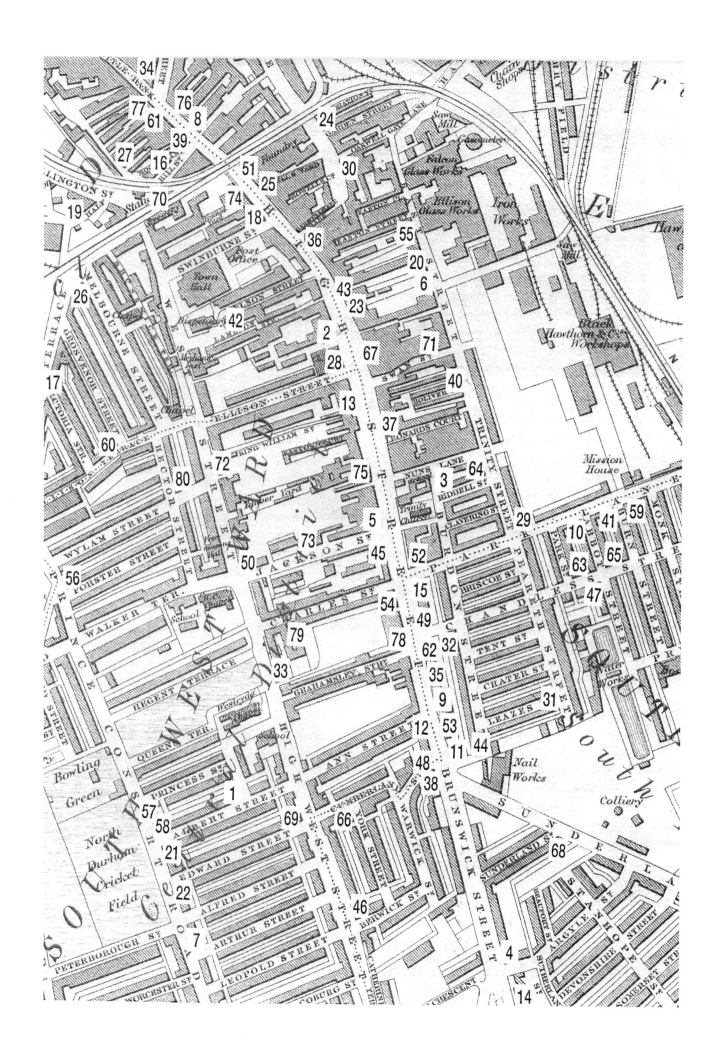

Pubs and beer-houses of central Gateshead

Less significant pubs, some early pubs and those built since 1939 have been excluded.

1. **Albert** (20 Albert St)
2. **Albion** (148 High St)
3. **Alma** (10 Nuns La)
4. **Argyle** (423 High St)
5. **Atlas** (244 High St)
6. **Barley Mow** (28 East St)
7. **Bee Hive** (67 Prince Consort Rd)
8. **Black Bull** (21 High St)
9. **Black Bull** (315 High St)
10. **Black Swan** (46 Park La)
11. **Blue Bell** (349 High St)
12. **British Lion** (318 High St)
13. **British Queen** (176 High St)
14. **Brunswick** (27 Old Durham Rd)
15. **Butchers' Arms** (257 High St)
16. **Central** (Half Moon La)
17. **Clavering Arms** (15a Mulgrave Tce)
18. **Coach and Horses** (76 High St)
19. **Commercial** (Half Moon La)
20. **Crawshay** (22 East St)
21. **Crichton Arms** (27 Prince Consort Rd)
22. **Cricketers' Arms** (39 Prince Consort Rd)
23. **Crown** (137 High St)
24. **Crystal Palace** (27 Oakwellgate)
25. **Dun Cow** (65 High St)
26. **Eagle** (7 Mulgrave Tce)
27. **Earl Grey** (Stobbs Yd, Mirk La)
28. **Ellison Arms** (164 High St)
29. **Ellison Arms** (33 Park La)
30. **Flying Horse** (31 Oakwellgate)
31. **Fountain** (29 Peareth St)
32. **Fox and Lamb** (1a Chandless St)
33. **Gloucester** (31 High West St)
34. **Goat** (39 Bottle Bank)
35. **Golden Fleece** (309 High St)
36. **Grey Horse** (99 High St)
37. **Grey Nag's Head** (219 High St)
38. **Grove** (332 High St)
39. **Half Moon** (2 and 30 Half Moon La)
40. **Hawks' Arms** (50 East St)
41. **Hutt's Arms** (62 Park La)
42. **Lord Nelson** (39 Nelson St)
43. **Lord Raglan** (137 High St)
44. **Masons' Arms** (101 Burdon St)
45. **Metropole** (246 High St)
46. **Neville** (123 High West St)
47. **Northumberland Arms** (55 Chandless St)
48. **O'Keefe's** (324 High St)
49. **Old Fleece** (289 High St)
50. **Old Mill** (113 West St)
51. **Old Nag's Head** (59 High St)
52. **Park House** (253 High St)
53. **Peareth Arms** (337 High St)
54. **Phoenix (Curley's)** (266 High St)
55. **Plough** (14 East St)
56. **Prince Albert** (2 Forster St)
57. **Prince Alfred** (17 Prince Consort Rd)
58. **Prince Consort** (25 Prince Consort Rd)
59. **Prince of Wales** (63 Chandless St)
60. **Princess of Wales** (16 Ellison St West)
61. **Queen's Head** (16 High St)
62. **Rector House** (293 High St)
63. **Richard Cobden** (40 Chandless St)
64. **Ridley Arms** (13 Riddell St)
65. **Royal Albert** (48 Chandless St)
66. **Scotch Arms** (16 Cumberland St)
67. **Ship** (169 High St)
68. **Shipcote** (32 Sunderland Rd)
69. **Star** (32 High West St)
70. **Station** (6 Hills St)
71. **Swan** (29 Swan St)
72. **Talbot** (61 West St)
73. **Tilley Stone** (9 Jackson St)
74. **Turk's Head** (68 High St)
75. **Waggon** (214 High St)
76. **Wheat Sheaf** (13 High St)
77. **William IV** (10 High St)
78. **William IV** (288 High St)
79. **Windmill** (39 Charles St)
80. **Wylam** (10 Wylam St)

An opening day advert for the Gloucester from 1963.

East Gateshead
Along the South Shore and Sunderland Road

Old Sunderland Road was the main route east from central Gateshead. The terracing either side was similar to that which followed other major roads, but the standard of most of the housing was superior to that on the High Street. Given the number of people living in the district, there were relatively few pubs. Most of these houses were built after 1869 when magistrates were given more powers to refuse licences and therefore had some control over where the town's future pubs could be located.

Just off Sunderland Road was the **Queen's Hotel**. With there being so many other similarly named 'Queen's' in the town, it more usually went by the name of 'the Bridge'. The Bridge did brisk trade from Clarke Chapman's Victoria works during the day with beers lined up ready for the influx of thirsty workers and a scramble to get drinks in by the 3 o'clock closing time. (The post-war **Old Fold Tavern** (p7) provided a similar service for Clarke Chapman's 'Power Engineering' workers.) The **Claxton Hotel** further down Sunderland Road, was also well patronised by workers from 'Clarkies' as many lived in the adjoining streets.

Two other East Gateshead pubs were well supported by local workers. The **Vulcan** on Quarry Field (Quarryfield) Road and the **Patent Hammer** on Hawks Road (p38) indicate the original local trades, but East Gateshead was and is home to many other businesses whose workers patronised these pubs in later days. (The nearby **Crystal Palace** in Oakwellgate drew similar trade.) The **Patent Hammer** did have a brief life after closure in 1982 when it re-opened for a short time as the **Great North Run**.

Between Sunderland Road and the river were a number of isolated communities. The Saltmeadows community supported several pubs over time, most recently the **Saltmeadows House** and confusingly two pubs with **Deptford** in their name. '**Spires Deptford**' aka the **Deptford** or the **New Deptford** (as opposed to **Deptford House**) was run by Herbert Spires and competed with the **Albert**, the **Burton House** and the **Golden Fleece** for the honour of being Gateshead's smallest pub.

The Queen's Hotel on St James Road around 1965.

The Vulcan around 1950.

The (New) Deptford around 1950.

The Claxton around 1960.

Slightly inland and built as a settlement for Hawks, Crawshay ironworkers was New Gateshead. The **New Gateshead Inn** had wooden benches and was a basic pub to say the least (p36). When it closed in the 1980s, it claimed to be the only 'Free House' in the town. It had been owned by both Newcastle and Gateshead Councils and run throughout its 150 year life by members of the Chisholm family (hence its nickname 'Chizzie's').

Riverside pubs abound with trade and nautical names as they would have served not only locals but those sailing up (or across) the Tyne as part of their work. The pubs included the **Lime Kiln**, the **Neptune**, the **White Bear** (previously the **Greenland Bear** p40) and of course the **Ship**. There were several 'Ships' along this stretch at one time – not very imaginative – and again very confusing! The current **Schooner** was one of these. Although the present building is a turn of the century rebuild, there has been a **Ship** on this site for well over 200 years. It was popularly known as 'the Bunk' most probably as it provided alternative accommodation for passing sailors although there are other explanations. Old pubs like old houses are often said to be haunted – a previous landlord is still said to reside at the **Ship/Schooner**.

The New Gateshead Inn around 1975.

The Ship (now the Schooner) in 1964.

Along the Old Durham Road
Mount Pleasant, Deckham, Sheriff Hill and Wrekenton

Our first pub away from the High Street was better known as 'Solly's' after the landlord John Solly. The **Brunswick Hotel** also had a shady third title: the 'Clickem', said to be a reference to success with women who frequented the snug! Like the nearby **British Lion**, it too had a freak in a glass case on display: in this case a dog with 8 legs 2 tails and one head (verified by the Solly family). The **Brunswick** was also the last pub on the long journey from funeral services at St Mary's Church to burial at East Gateshead Cemetery. As many early journeys were made on foot, it was not unknown for pallbearers to leave the coffin on the pavement as they took on much needed refreshment inside.

The Brunswick Hotel around 1965.

Official and unofficial names are as old as pubs; modern names for the next pubs south included **Maxwell Plum's** for the **Globe** and **Annie O'Hagan's** and **Sloppy Joe's** for the **Cross House Hotel** just round the corner. The **Cross House** is unusual in Gateshead with its tower and particularly its terracotta tiling and was rebuilt around 1900 at a time when the Mount Pleasant area had become relatively affluent.

The **Deckham Hotel** was located near the junction of Split Crow Road and survived into the 21st century. It was formerly a beer-house called the

The Globe on Old Durham Road around 1950.

Gate but in 1879 upgraded to a fully licensed ale-house and changed its name. Off Split Crow Road and further into the Mount Pleasant district, we still find a **Shakespeare**, rebuilt in the 1960s to replace the old beer-house in the picture opposite. Beyond that was the **Cromwell**, nicknamed 'Della's' for a while – presumably after a landlady.

Cross House (as Annie O'Hagan's) in 1990.

The Deckham in 1982.

Back on the Old Durham Road we are reminded how agricultural this area would have been before Victorian times. We still have the **Plough** (p40 – originally 'Speed the Plough'). Going further back in history you could also quench your thirst at the nearby **Wheat Sheaf** and further south at the **Shepherd and Shepherdess** (Blue Quarries).

In the 1800s Carr Hill was an isolated village where there were mills, brick, glass, quarrying and pottery works. The village inns were (**Ye Olde**) **Brown Jug** (p38) and the **Gardeners' Arms** (originally the **Free Gardeners' Arms** and at one time the **Oddfellows' Arms**).

As old Gateshead was cleared it was the open land around such villages that was built on for replacement housing. Traditional occupations died out but the pubs were given a new lease of life by the arrival of new residents and many of the old pubs in this area were rebuilt. In the present era these neighbourhood 'locals' seemed to have had the most difficulty surviving. On closure, the more usual fate has been to adapt the premises as houses or flats as with the **Brown Jug** and the nearby **Swan** (traditionally the **White Swan**), or clearance of the site for new building (as with the **Gardeners' Arms** – although this followed a fire).

The Shakespeare around 1955.

The Cromwell in 1977.

Four Sheriff Hill pubs stand relatively close together on the Old Durham Road: the **Old Cannon**, the **Queen's Head**, the **Three Tuns** and the **Travellers' Rest** reminding us that this was once also part of the 'Great North Road'.

The **Travellers' Rest** (p38) has undergone a few changes of name in its time. It was previously a beer-house and remembered as the **Quoit** or **Golden Quoit** after its old quoits pit. In the 1980s it styled itself the **Crofters**. Along with all the pubs on Sheriff Hill it is known to have supported local leek shows.

The old **Three Tuns** was a pub patronised by miners and quarrymen. A newspaper article of 1891 describes its early life as a sportsman's pub, home to cuddy racing and cockfighting and where a Jenny Hall ran the 'Women's Box' benefit club, collecting weekly contributions at the pub for help in times of sickness or need.

Jenny Hall's tale shows us the important role played by such pubs in local communities; this could also be said of the **Queen's Head** (see also p2) where they have been able to host large gatherings for over 150 years.

The Queen's Head on Sheriff Hill around 1900.

The Causeway around 1970.

The Gardeners' Arms on Carr Hill Road in 1984.

Traditionally the **Old Cannon** (pp38-39) was the most select of the Sheriff Hill inns. From medieval times Assize Judges from Durham coming north would meet the Sheriff of Northumberland coming south to discuss the more serious legal issues in the two counties. They did so at the **Old Cannon** and 'Sheriff Hill' takes its name from this meeting.

Much of the land south of here was developed after the war and a number of new estate pubs built. There is a listing of post-war pubs on page 47.

Wrekenton began as a village in the 1820s after local land was bought up ('enclosed') and local people moved to where the 'Great North Road' crosses the Wrenkendyke Roman road.

Before the enclosures there were only three inns over the High Fell, the (Old) **Cannon**, the **Three Tuns** and the **Seven Stars**. The **Seven Stars** bears an unusual name. Both the **Princess Alice** and the **Seven Stars** were originally located on Pleiad Place. 'Pleiad' is a particular cluster of seven stars that can be seen with the naked eye. The **Princess Alice** was demolished when much of old Wrekenton was pulled down between 1938 and 1940; as can be seen from the picture on page 35 the **Seven Stars** was rebuilt.

The Three Tuns around 1900.

The (White) Swan in 1977.

Three pubs stand very close together in the centre of Wrekenton: the **Royal Oak**, the **Half Moon** and the **Coach and Horses**. For a number of years the **Half Moon** closed completely, but in 2006 reopened in part of the former building as the **Clock**. The corner and portion on Wrekenton Row is currently used by a bookmaker.

One of the older pubs in the district is the **Coach and Horses**. This was used as a stopping place for the mail coach up until 1844 (when the railways took over) and known at the time as 'Red Robin's'.

Robert Stephenson wore a bright red waistcoat with his publican's apron hence the naming. His son, also Robert ran the **Three Tuns** on Sheriff Hill, sported the same attire and went by the name of 'Red Bob'. Red Robin came to a particularly sad end: beaten to death with his own crutch whilst disturbing a burglar.

Going back fifty years or so, the **Seven Stars** is remembered as the pigeon fanciers' pub managed by an ex-seaman who kept a monkey from his travels behind the bar. Two members of the Dixon family give us a portrait of the pub scene at the time: '*You were lucky to get out on a Saturday (for financial reasons), but most would go on Sunday mornings. Most pitmen were club men (Stormont Main) but pitmen were the main folk to use the pubs too as the main employment was pits with some quarry workers and a couple of farmers. People went where their mates went and just followed each other. You had to be working to get beer. There were very few women – only behind the bar serving. They would usually be in the house watching the children. Women in bars were frowned upon and it was* a man's domain in the main. However, a few of the older women may have had a gill and then gone home as opposed to staying all evening!'

The Royal Oak and Half Moon around 1910.

The Princess Alice around 1925.

At the time it was the **Royal Oak** and **Half Moon** that had the worst reputation for trouble. The **Half Moon** had staff better able to control this, but … '*The local policeman knew everyone. Any trouble and the person would be taken home to family or he would just hit them as opposed to arresting them. He ended up as a School Board man. Whilst on duty as a policeman, he would have a gill or a half in every pub whilst checking. He wouldn't drink at the main bar; he would use the snug. The snug was very small and used by older people. 10 in and it would be full!'*

The pattern we noted in Carr Hill seems also to be true of Wrekenton: pubs have survived better on main roads and in centres. Recent 'outlying' pubs that have closed include the **Ship** and the post-war **Wrekendike** although the rebuilt **Springwell Inn** continues to do business on the very edge of the Gateshead Borough boundaries.

The Ship at Wrekenton around 1985.

Low Fell

Although modern Low Fell is centred on the Durham Road, the new thoroughfare was only completed in the 1820s. The road and the enclosure mentioned previously stimulated Low Fell's development and it grew to become a relatively affluent Victorian suburb.

Low Fell remains almost as it was built. Its location and more solid construction means it has avoided re-development and there have been fewer recent changes in Low Fell's pubs scene than any other part of the town.

Pubs and (pub names) have been lost to the district though and the old Trade Directories list the **Bee Hive** (which was just east of St Helen's Church), the **Engine/Steam Engine** (bottom of Engine Lane), the **Moulders' Arms** (next to the **Belle Vue**), the **Old Angel**, the **Queen Adelaide**, the **Rake and Spade/Rake and Shovel** (north side of the Belle Vue Bank/ Durham Road corner) and the **Sun** (on the 'Glenbrooke' site, Chowdene Bank).

The Buck (now Beaconsfield) around 1900.

Two lost names were known as previous titles for existing pubs. The **Buck** pictured above was to become the **Beaconsfield Arms**, and the **Queen's Head** became the **Victoria** (p34).

It is probable that the **Sovereign** became the **George IV** and possible that the **Queen Adelaide** was an early name for the **Victoria**. There may also be links between the **Belle Vue** (which took over the **Moulders' Arms** licence) and the earlier **Cross Keys** as they are both on Cross Keys Lane but the earlier inn was 100 yards off the main road.

The New Cannon around 1910.

When Robert Clements realised that the new road through Low Fell was going to take passing trade from his inn on Old Durham Road, he opened a new one on the corner of Beaconsfield Road and called it the **New Cannon**. His instincts served him well as this was always a major Low Fell meeting point for social gatherings, dinners, concerts and meetings.

The **Gateshead Arms** is also written up in the local press as a meeting point for local groups. It housed meetings of the 'Association for the Prosecution of Felons' as well as the prestigious Dahlia show in 1837. In times past, this pub also went by the nickname of the 'Grapes' as it was a meeting place for gardeners from the grand houses where grape growing was greatly in fashion. A more recent experience was as a 'modern' makeover under the name **Smart**. This was not a success and the **Gateshead Arms** quickly returned to a traditional style.

The Crown at Low Fell around 1950.

Scottish widow Jane McKie was a licensee for over 20 years at the **George IV**. This formidable multi-tasking lady helped develop property in adjoining streets ('Kie's' corner is an old name for where the **George IV** stands) and combined her landlady duties with those of an 'Omnibus Proprietress'. During these last years of the 19th century work would have started on moving from the old single-story inn to new premises on the opposite (south) side of Hutton Terrace.

According to historian Clarence Walton the Black Horse probably has the honour of calling itself the oldest pub in the town (within its original building) and the adjoining Lowrey's Lane is almost certainly named after a previous landlord (Thomas Lowrey). Low Fell pubs feature several times in the poetry of Thomas Wilson. In the 'Pitman's Pay' (1843) he describes the **Black Horse** as a venue 'for cock-fighting, cuddy racing and all other pitmen's amusements on the pay nights' and the delightfully titled 'Oiling of Dicky's Wig' (1826) tells of the first stage coach trip along Low Fell's new turnpike road. As part of their celebrations the travellers paid a visit to the four new inns that had been granted licences. These were the '**Ship**', the '**Cannon**', the '**Engine**' and the '**Sov'reign**'.

The Gateshead Arms around 1910.

The Belle Vue around 1910.

The Black Horse around 1950.

The George IV in 1968.

33

Part Three
Insides, Outsides, Brewers, Owners and Names
Putting on the style: Gateshead pub architecture

Look around at any Gateshead pub and it will have been built in a particular style. This style will reflect when it was built, where it was built, why it was built, who built it and how much money they spent. This cannot be an exhaustive listing but here are eight local pub styles, examples of which can still be seen in our town today.

Traditional Northumbrian

The Victoria at Low Fell around 1920.

Stone built, simple in style and often detached. Most commonly found in outlying districts or where there has been less re-development. The **Victoria** in Low Fell and the **Borough Arms** on Bensham Road (p21) are two good examples of the detached and traditional; the **Gateshead Arms** (p33) of a traditional pub attached to a terrace. Many pubs in this early style were lost having been replaced by rebuilds in a more national style.

Corner Houses

This was the most typical Gateshead pub from the Victorian period. They were often built as part of the new housing development, were superior to the terraced bar and capable of capturing business on two streets. These corner pubs were a big feature of the terraces that ran off Gateshead's main highways such as the High Street, East Street, Prince Consort, Askew and Bensham Roads. They were also common in terraced districts such as Chandless as with the **Northumberland Arms**. On the High Street, the **Rector House** and the **Old Fleece** (both p14) belong to this style. The most quirky corner house was probably 'the Coffin' on Derwentwater Road; although its Sunday name was the **Foresters' Arms** (see front and back covers).

Mid Terrace

The Golden Fleece around 1950.

Many of Gateshead's beer-houses would have been of this style as these properties were at the poorer end of the market. Many were converted dwelling houses consisting of no more a single room in which to serve customers. The **Golden Fleece** on the High Street and the **Princess Alice** at Wrekenton (p31) are the best examples in this survey. However terracing did not always mean a poorer establishment, especially if the location was on a major road instead of a side street. We can see this in the case of the **Crown** ('tap@carter's well') in Low Fell (p32).

The Northumberland Arms about 1920.

Georgian extensions

The Crown on Coatsworth Road around 1910.

The Victorians were fond of these. Take a Georgian building and add a flat roofed, single storey, curved extension. A very typical Gateshead style, still to be seen with the **William IV** and **Curley's**/the **Phoenix** (High Street) and also the **Crown**, above.

Tudorbethan rebuilds

The Seven Stars around 1950.

This was the most common style for replacing pubs either side of the Great War when many traditional stone built pubs disappeared. Wooden beams were a favourite feature as can be seen on the **Seven Stars** at Wrekenton and the **George IV** ('Aletaster') in Low Fell (p33).

Post-clearance pubs

The book title might suggest 'old' pubs meaning 'traditional' pubs, but as several of the newer pubs have now closed, these now become 'historical' in their own way! Unsurprisingly the heyday of post-war building was around the 1960s when new pubs in new areas were provided for re-housed residents from the clearance districts. The **British Queen** on Split Crow Road reflects the house style of the time.

Right: The British Queen in 1982.

Grand Hotels

The Royal in 1969.

A grander architecture was used to impress the public and attract the more discerning patron to an establishment, although for the size of the town, Gateshead has had comparatively few of these. We can see the ideas used in designs for the **Royal** on Prince Consort Road, the **Metropole** (p13) and **Crown** (p42) on the High Street and the **Half Moon Hotel** (p10).

Art Deco and Interwar re-builds

The Star Hotel around 1950.

A few older pubs were re-built during this period in the clean-lined style often associated with cinema building. Prominent among them were the **Star** on West Street, the **Argyle** (p15) on the High Street and the present **New Cannon** in Low Fell (a 1937 rebuild).

Bars, Lounges, Saloons and Snugs
Inside the old pubs of Gateshead

By far the most common interior arrangement for an old Gateshead pub was of two rooms served by a central bar. Even the smallest of these pubs such as the **Golden Fleece** and the **Albert** are remembered as having a second room. Single roomed drinking establishments certainly existed, but these are likely to have been in older beer-houses.

The two roomed model provided for a public bar and what might be termed a lounge, a saloon or a snug. The bar provided space for the working man where dress didn't matter, where he could be himself (this was usually a 'men only' zone) and where the cheapest drinks could be had. Accompanied women could be accommodated in the other room where work clothes would not be worn, where furnishings would be more comfortable and where you would expect to pay a little more for your drinks.

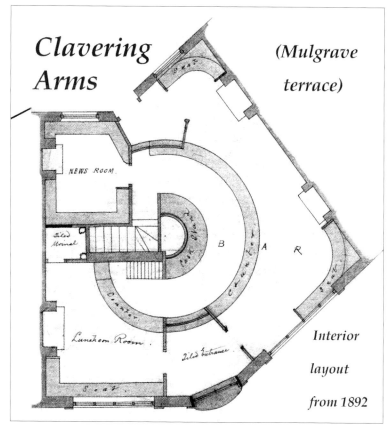

Clavering Arms (Mulgrave terrace)

Interior layout from 1892

At the New Gateshead Inn around 1975.

At the Grey Nag's Head in 1959.

It was usual for pubs to provide off sales and many had separate 'Jug and Bottle' departments (as can be seen on the floor plan for the **Waggon**). Often the size of cubby holes and no more, these would be where women in particular could discreetly buy a jug of beer for their husband back home (or themselves). Access was usually from the street so purchases need not be observed from inside. Society's rules on women and pubs did change over time, but 'men only' bars and taboos on pub visits by unaccompanied women survived well into the late 20th century.

The larger pubs had extra space and often extra rooms. A number had extensive rooms on the first floor which could be used for meetings, concerts, wedding receptions or just as on overflow when the occasion demanded it. The **Metropole** and the **Queen's Head** (High Street), the **Queen's Head** (Sheriff Hill), the **New Cannon** (Low Fell) and the **Five Wand Mill** (Bensham Road) provide just a small sample of examples.

Every pub went through design changes as managers and owners tried to catch the latest mood and win new business. At the top end of the market, great expense was lavished to improve the reputation of pubs as suitable places to visit and at all levels money was spent to make the pub a warmer and more desirable place than locals might have to experience back home. This was all business. There was no sentimentality if a change in décor was seen as necessary and many a piece of carved Edwardian woodwork gave way to streamlined plastic and plywood. Early pub users liked the privacy of screens, but these were mostly swept away between the wars when a more open plan was preferred. This clean-lined, uncluttered open approach was popular through until at least the 1960s although ornaments and a fuller decoration have become more acceptable in recent decades as 'old pub' nostalgia has grown.

It is unusual still to find a pub still trading in its separate rooms although these can still be found at the **Three Tuns** on Sheriff Hill and the **Belle Vue** in Low Fell. Better visibility for bar staff and a less class conscious society mean that one open space is now the order of the day.

As part of a rebranding many old pubs have tried a modern approach looking to hook in the young and the 'trend conscious'. The **Crown** in Low Fell still trades under a modern name, but many have reverted to their historic names and have tried to recapture the traditional pub atmosphere in their decor.

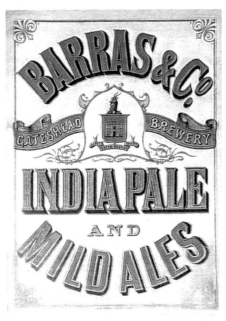

An advert for Barras Pale Ale.

Blue Bell bar staff around 1910.

At the Dun Cow around 1950.

'Why's it called that?' – Pub names in Gateshead

Pubs take names to attract custom and brand themselves as distinctive. Frequently they celebrate locations, trades, people or events and sometimes they make use of existing names already celebrated in their street as with **Nelson**, **Ellison** or the **Honeysuckle** off Woodbine Terrace (a Woodbine is a wild Honeysuckle).

Pubs have always changed names to keep 'up to date': the late **Moon and Sixpence** (traditionally the **British Lion** on the High Street), **Annie O'Hagan's** (**Cross House** on Cross Street) and the **Aletaster** (**George IV** in Low Fell) are mutations with a long tradition.

Local Trades and Industries

The **Patent Hammer** on Hawks Road, the **Vulcan** on Quarry Field Road, the **Hawks' Arms** and the **Crawshay** on East Street were all located near to the ironworks of Hawks, Crawshay and John Abbot and Co. The **Brown Jug** on Sheriff Hill celebrates the nearby pottery industry.

Earlier inn history is littered with examples of former Gateshead trades as we discover the **Boiler Makers' Arms** on Oakwellgate Chare, the **Cork Cutters' Arms** on Rabbit Banks, the **Glass Makers' Arms** on Pipewellgate, the **Lime Kiln** on the South Shore Road and the **Locomotive** on Ellison Street West.

The Patent Hammer around 1950.

The Travellers' Rest around 1975.

The Brown Jug in 1983.

Transport

Road travellers were enticed to stop and tarry at the **Coach and Horses** in Wrekenton or the **Travellers' Rest** on Old Durham Road, rail users by the **Brandling Junction** on Pipewellgate and the **Station** on Hills Street and even those travelling up the Tyne might be sorely tempted to visit the **Steamboat** on Church Street or one of several **Ships** (South Shore or Tyne Main).

Celebrities

Askew Arms on Askew Road. The Askew family owned the Redheugh estate from the mid 1700s to the 1880s and lived at nearby Redheugh Hall.

Old Cannon on Sheriff Hill. There are two possibilities for this one. Just maybe it should be spelt 'Canon' after the visiting clerics from Durham described on page 30. It is also said that cannons were fired to celebrate the occasion. You choose!

Clavering Arms on Mulgrave Terrace. The Claverings were an important local family who owned Axwell Hall near Blaydon.

Richard Cobden on Chandless Street. Richard Cobden was an MP (though not local) and a radical political hero.

The Old Cannon around 1950.

The Ellison Arms on the High Street around 1950.

Crawshay on East Street. The Crawshays were ironmasters and business partners in the firm Hawks, Crawshay. Family interests ranged from Gateshead to South Wales to France.

Curley's on the High Street (traditionally the **Phoenix**). The pub was run by boxer Will Curley whose winnings and fame allowed him to support a new living (pp14-15).

Ellison Arms on Ellison Street and Park Lane. Cuthbert Ellison was MP for Newcastle, High Sheriff of Durham and lived at Park House in East Gateshead (incorporated into Clarke Chapman's Victoria Works until closure).

Hawks' Arms on East Street. The Hawks family were a dynasty of Gateshead ironmasters and major local employers. George Hawks was Gateshead's first mayor in 1836.

Hutt's Arms on Park Lane. William Hutt was Gateshead's MP for over 30 years.

Will Curley, Gateshead Boxer.

The Phoenix (later Curley's) around 1985.

Neville Hotel on High West Street. Samuel Neville was a Gateshead glassworks owner who had bought land near this pub. Possible alternative: the aristocratic Neville family owned land in the Birtley area.

Ridley Arms on Riddell Street. Although the Ridley family have North East connections, the pub stood on Riddell Street – part of the land occupied by Gateshead House/Hall, the home of Sir Thomas Riddell. This sounds like a case of confusion at naming time!

Left: The Ridley Arms in 1959.

Birds and Animals

Local angles to the traditional use of animal names could add that extra prestige.

The **Dun Cow** (on the High Street – 'Dun' means brown) is supposed to have led the monks carrying St Cuthbert's coffin to Durham where the Cathedral now stands.

The **Goat** on Bottle Bank was previously called the **Bell of the Hoop** and the **Spread Eagle**. It was re-named in 1672 – probably after the popular belief that Goat was the origin of the town's name.

The old name for a **Magpie** (on Derwentwater Road) was a pianet, and Pianet Place was located in the Teams. The magpie was considered a bird of good omen and a good chatterer – not an unsuitable name for a pub!

Lastly, at Saltmeadows there was an inn called the **White Bear** (formerly the **Greenland Bear**). The riverside is known to have supported businesses related to the whaling industry. We can presume this naming is connected with shipping interests in far off places.

The Dun Cow (right and the Old Nag's Head, left) around 1900.

The Crystal Palace around 1965.

The Plough on Old Durham Road around 1950.

Unusual but Interesting ...

The **Alma** on Nuns Lane (see front cover) was probably named after the Battle of the Alma in the Crimean War of 1854. The surrounding streets were built in the same period.

The **Crystal Palace** on Oakwellgate traded as the **Royal Oak** until the 1850s. We may assume that the owners wished to identify with the successful exhibition in London.

The **Windmill** on Charles Street, the **Old Mill** on West Street and the **Five Wand Mill** on Bensham Road all celebrate the traditional windmills of the town (still remembered, of course, in the district of Windmill Hills.)

The **Causeway** on Blue Quarries Road celebrated local quarrying and the nearby Roman Road.

The **Barley Mow** on East Street and the **Plough** (East Street and Old Durham Road) reflect the fact that until recent building these areas would have been agricultural land.

The **Claxton** on Sunderland Road was named after a small estate east of the Old Durham Road.

Brewers and Owners

In earlier days most inns and taverns in Gateshead were independent establishments brewing their own beer. Bridge Street examples included the **Queen's Arms** and the **Blue Bell** and on the High Street the **Grey Nag's Head** and the **British Lion**. There also existed 'Common Brewers' brewing on behalf of others and by 1900 most beer was brewed in this way. Early 'Common Brewers' included the Hillgate Brewery (run by the Hepple family) and the Oakwellgate Brewery (McLeod and Sons). Later Victorian breweries included the Ellison Street Brewery and Dawson and Company's Vulcan Brewery, both on or near the High Street. Three Gateshead brewers stand out in the town's history as major enterprises serving not only Gateshead people, but other north-eastern towns as well. These were the breweries of Barras, Tucker and Rowell.

John Barras and Co

John Barras was from a wealthy Whickham family and in the 1770s acquired premises for a brewery in the modern Swinburne Street area. His son John Jnr (a Gateshead Mayor) developed and expanded the business but had no suitable sons to take over. Control passed to a relative by marriage although the Barras name continued to

JOHN BARRAS & CO.,
BREWERS OF THE
CELEBRATED MILD ALES,
AND MALTSTERS.
THE OLD BREWERY,
60, HIGH ST. & WEST ST.,
GATESHEAD.

A John Barras and Co advert.   *John Barras Jnr.*

be used. In 1884 a replacement Newcastle site was secured as the firm outgrew its Gateshead premises (called the 'Old Brewery'). In 1890, John Barras and Co amalgamated with four other local concerns to become the Newcastle Breweries Ltd.

Isaac Tucker and Co Ltd

The Turk's Head Brewery was established in 1790, but Isaac Tucker himself only became involved at a later date. He was succeeded in the business by his son, Thomas in whose 1891 obituary it is recorded that the firm employed 100 men and 40 horses. The firm took over James Robinson and Son Ltd, wine and spirit merchants in 1932 but was itself taken over in 1967 by Whitbread and Co. On closure, Tucker's had 30 employees and 50 tied houses. The brewery buildings were demolished in 1970. Both Tucker's and the former Barras Brewery lay between the High Street and West Street. The area was cleared from around 1970 in preparation for a new road.

Tucker's Brewery around 1965.

Tucker's (Turk's Head) Brewery entrance around 1950.

John Rowell and Son Ltd

John Rowell founded the 'New Brewery' on Gateshead's High Street in 1840. Around the turn of the century the business expanded as Rowell's took over the businesses of J.M. Bruce, Wm. Turnbull and Co of South Shields, Gilpin and Co of Gateshead and Matthew Taylor and Co of Swalwell. The 'Gateshead Breweries Corporation' was added in 1912. The 'New Brewery' underwent a major refurbishment in 1913. Gilpin's works on East Street provided bottling capacity with the main offices and the **Crown Hotel** on the High Street. In 1935, Rowell's tried unsuccessfully to take over local rivals Tucker's and in 1959 was itself taken over by the Newcastle Breweries. Operations in Gateshead were wound up in 1960 and the site later demolished.

An advert for John Rowell and Son.

Rowell's Brewery Headquarters and Crown Hotel around 1960.

Other Brewers and Owners

As was noted in the introduction, the 1869 Wine and Beer House Act began a major rethink in the attitude of brewers and other pub owners. Magistrates had the power to deny licences and later close pubs, so protecting these outlets became a business imperative. Breweries and other interested businesses such as bottlers and wine and spirit merchants began buying up pubs and creating 'estates'. This trend can be seen in the Trade Directory listings on pages 44 to 47.

A further trend on the brewing and ownership scene came as a result of rail development. 'Newcastle Mild' was the traditional local brew; dark, sweet and a reflection of local water quality. Rail development opened up the north-east market to light, clear and better quality beers particularly from London, Burton and Scotland and these brewers also joined in the pub purchase game.

Brewers from outside the region established agents here and sometimes breweries. Local brewers and other pub-owning concerns fought back by themselves becoming agents and adapting their product to changing local tastes.

The trend from late Victorian times is one of ever progressing amalgamations as A was taken over by B who in turn was taken over by C. The trend also goes from district brewer to town brewer to regional to national and is currently international. Microbreweries such as the Big Lamp at Newburn have returned us to grass roots at one level, but to date no shoots have appeared in central Gateshead.

The ownership saga is too complicated and too long-winded to outline here, but names no longer with us appear in connection with the old pubs in Trade Directories, on photographs and in people's memories. I hope these brief notes help provide a little more understanding.

Archibald Arrol and Sons Ltd were Alloa brewers who also owned a number of Tyneside pubs. They were taken over by *Allsopp's*, (Burton brewers and also Gateshead pub owners). Arrol houses in Gateshead included the **Alma**, the **British Lion** and the **Victoria** (St Cuthberts Road aka the **Underhand**).

Robert Deuchar Ltd did own a brewery in Sandyford, although in later years chose to bring beers by rail from the Duddingston Brewery near Edinburgh. Gateshead pubs included the **Albert**, the **Black Bull** (Mulgrave Terrace) and the **Crystal Palace**.

James Deuchar arrived on Tyneside from Scotland and was publican at the **Argyle Hotel** in the late 1860s. In time he built up a large estate of north-eastern pubs and bought the Lochside Brewery in Montrose. Using his own steam ships he supplied Tyneside and beyond with his Lochside beers. Gateshead pubs included the **Argyle**, the **Golden Fleece** and the **Grey Nag's Head**. Newcastle Breweries Ltd took over *Robert Deuchar Ltd* in 1953 and *James Deuchar Ltd* in 1956.

An advert for Lochside's Beer from around 1930.

H. Fail and Co was a Tyneside pub owning firm based in Gateshead and closely associated with John Rowell and Son Ltd. Henry Fail was manager at the **Honeysuckle Hotel** on Coatsworth Road and other Fail houses were at the **Globe** (Old Durham Road), the **Neville** and the **Barley Mow**. Rowell's began to use their own name for Fail pubs after the late 1920s.

Davison and Wood went into partnership in 1893 as publicans and wine and spirit merchants with registered office and stores on West Street (and King William Street). They continued in business until 1959 when they sold to Nimmo's of Castle Eden (soon to become part of Whitbread and Co). The D and W initials appeared distinctively over their flagship premises, the **Half Moon Hotel** (p10) until demolition in the new millennium. A list of their pubs appears in the advert on this page.

Swinburne and Co were also Gateshead wine and spirit merchants and had originally been brewers. Their chain of pubs included at one time most of the larger and grander establishments in the town including the **Royal Hotel**, the **Queen's Hotel** (St James Road) and the **Central**. Swinburne and Co were one of the companies that amalgamated in 1890 to become the Newcastle Breweries Ltd.

Robinson and Anderson. Thomas 'Tot' Anderson (senior) was publican at the **William IV** (off Bottle Bank) which closed in the late 1930s after which the family moved across the road to the **Old Nag's Head**. Tot joined in partnership with bookmaker Alec Robinson, but seems to have been the driving force in the business. The firm were installed as tenants in the pubs of *James Calder and Co* and owned several of their own including the **Plough** on East Street. Tot was a Gateshead personality and his funeral cortege is shown leaving the **William IV** for St Mary's Church in 1936.

Above: The funeral cortege of Gateshead pub owner 'Tot' Anderson in 1936. The coffin is leaving Tot's own pub the William IV (right) for St Mary's Church. Further up Bottle Bank/High Street (left) can be seen the Queen's Head.

Right: An advert for Davison and Wood.

Telephone 71581

DAVISON & WOOD LTD.
Wine and Spirit Merchants
GATESHEAD

QUALITY
WINES and SPIRITS
DRAUGHT and BOTTLED
ALES and STOUTS

LOCAL HOUSES

Beaconsfield Hotel	Golden Fleece
Brown Jug Inn	Lambton Arms
Cross House	Peareth Arms
Half Moon Hotel (LOW BAR)	Rector House
Half Moon Hotel (HIGH BAR)	Stirling House
Talbot Hotel	

Directory and Index of Old Pubs

Please note that this is neither a full list of all the pubs in Gateshead nor a full index to this book. It is a record of entries appearing in selected local Trade Directories between 1889 and 1939. These have been used as the basis for an index to the pages on which the pub or beer-house is mentioned in the book. The last Trade Directory to cover Gateshead fully was 1939. A listing from 1889 to 1939 has kept content manageable, but still includes those Gateshead pubs that survived into the modern era. Users do need to recognize the limitations of Trade Directories. Absence does not mean a pub or beer-house did not exist. Businesses paid to be included and most beer-houses did not advertise. This is why beer-house entries are marked * – their entries are less useful as an indicator of lifespan. Please note also that the date given is the year the Directory was published and not the dates the pub was built!

The addresses and names given vary enormously. Addresses chosen are the most recent provided and for only the first number is used where properties cover several (e.g. 20-22 High Street).

For each entry additional information is given as follows:

1) The second street for corner pubs is listed where they can be traced on maps in the Gateshead Library collection (I felt this would be useful to readers).

2) To help readers appreciate the lifespan of a pub the codes f.e. and l.e. have been used. f.e. = first entry and l.e. = last entry. This indicates the first and the last times that these pubs appear in all the Trade Directories below. This includes not only those from 1889 to 1939 used already, but also those from the earlier period.

3) Where a change of trading name is known of, this has been included as a help to the user.

4) (BH) means that on at least one occasion an entry has been described as a beer-house (or sometimes beer retailer). See above for reasons why beer-houses are marked *.

5) The listing of corporate owners given at the end of an entry is as recorded in the Ward's Directories of Newcastle and Gateshead for 1889 to 1939. (Kelly's Directories tended to record managers rather than owners but it is rarely clear if Directory entries refer to owners, licensees or other).

Additional Trade Directories used to help identify a pub's lifespan: 1782(NG), 1790(WH), 1811(MD), 1828(PW), 1833(I), 1838(R), 1844(WI), 1847(WT), 1850(W), 1851(H), 1856(WN), 1858(K), 1859(W), 1865(WN), 1869(W), 1874(C), 1879(W), 1886(K)

Trade Directories used to compile the list below: 1889(W), 1893(W), 1894(WN), 1899(W), 1905(W), 1906(K), 1909(W), 1913(W), 1918(W), 1925 (W), 1925 (K), 1929(W), 1933(W), 1938(K) and 1939(W).

Code to Directory publishers: NG = Newcastle and Gateshead, WH = Whitehead, MD = Mackenzie and Dent, PW = Parson's and White, I = Ihler, R = Richardson, WI = Williams, WT = White, W = Ward, H = Hagar, WN = Whellan, K = Kelly C = Christie

All entries are taken from the listings of trades except for 1782 and 1790 (tradesmen) and 1886 (streets). All these Directories and more can be found at Gateshead Library.

Albert (20 Albert St/Chapel St) *f.e.1879 (possibly 1874) R. Deuchar Ltd (f.e.1909)* **See pages 5, 20, 26, 43**
Albion (148 High St) *f.e.1847 Bell Bros (f.e.1905) Sir J. Fitzgerald Ltd (f.e.1925)* **See page 12**
Aletaster see **George IV**
Alma (10 Nuns La/Hopper St) *f.e.1869* **See front cover and pages 40, 42**
Argyle (423 High St/Argyle St) *f.e.1874 J. Deuchar Ltd (f.e.1889)* **See pages 15, 35, 43**
Askew Arms (120 Askew Rd/George St) *f.e.1874 Swinburne and Co (f.e.1905) Newcastle Breweries Ltd (f.e.1933)* **See pages 21, 38**
Atlas (244 High St/Jackson St) *f.e.1828 Swinburne and Co (f.e.1899) Newcastle Breweries Ltd (f.e.1933)* **See pages 14, 15**

Barge (4 Hillgate) *f.e.1790 l.e.1918 Davison and Wood (f.e.1899 l.e.1918)*
Barley Mow (28 East St) *f.e.1869 H. Fail and Co (f.e.1909) J. Rowell and Son Ltd (f.e.1939)* **See pages 16, 20, 40, 43**
Bath (16 Oakwellgate) *f.e.1879 (1856 as **Brewery Inn**) l.e.1909*
Beaconsfield (320 Askew Rd West) *f.e.1894 Davison and Wood Ltd (f.e.1899)* **See pages 21, 22**
Beaconsfield (5 Beaconsfield Rd, Low Fell) *f.e.1899 (1828 as **Buck**) J.G. Radcliffe/J.G. Radcliffe Ltd (f.e.1925) I. Tucker and Co Ltd (f.e.1939)* **See page 32**
Bee Hive (Primrose Pl, Belle Vue Bank, Low Fell) *f.e.1847 l.e.1918* **See page 32**
Bee Hive (BH) (67 Prince Consort Rd/Arthur St) *f.e.1886** **See page 20**
Belle Vue (538 Durham Rd, Low Fell) *f.e.1874 Wears and Watson/J.P.T. Wears (f.e.1913)* **See pages 32, 33, 37**
Bensham Jockey see **Ravensworth**
Bird (BH) (39 Oakwellgate) *f.e.1886 l.e.1894**
Black Bull (BH) (315 High St) *f.e.1869**
Black Bull (3, Freemans Pl, Mulgrave Tce) *f.e.1838 R. Deuchar Ltd (f.e.1899)* **See pages 18, 19, 20, 43**
Black Horse (Kells La, Low Fell) *f.e.1828 Newcastle Breweries Ltd (f.e.1929)* **See pages 4, 33**
Black Swan/Swan (46 Park La/Abbot St) *f.e.1869 H. Fail and Co (f.e.1899) J. Rowell and Son Ltd (f.e.1925)* **See page 17**
Blue Bell (10 Bridge St) *f.e.1828 (possibly 1790 as Bottle Bank) l.e.1905* **See page 41**
Blue Bell (349 High St) *f.e.1879 (1874 as **Brewers' Arms**) H. Fail and Co (f.e.1899) J. Rowell and Son Ltd (f.e.1925)* **See pages 14, 15, 37**
Board House (27 High St) *f.e.1889 l.e.1909 Davison and Wood f.e.1899 l.e.1909*
Borough Arms (BH) (82 Bensham Rd) *f.e.1838* *Swinburne and Co (f.e.1899) Newcastle Breweries Ltd (f.e.1933)* **See pages 5, 21, 34**
Brandling Junction (157 Pipewellgate) *f.e.1847 l.e.1909 Hewett and Golightly (f.e.1909)* **See page 38**
Brandy Vaults (25 Church St) *f.e.1844 l.e.1906*
Brass Mann/Brassman (23 Church St) *f.e.1886 l.e.1906*
Bridge (Pipewellgate) *f.e.1906*

British Lion (318 High Street/Ann St) *f.e.1859 A. Arrol and Sons Ltd (f.e.1899) Various from 1918*
   See pages 14, 15, 38, 41, 42
British Queen (176 High St) *f.e.1865 A. Arrol and Sons Ltd (f.e.1939)* **See page 12**
Brown Jug/Jug/Old Brown Jug/Ye Old Brown Jug (Carr Hill Rd) *f.e.1828 J.G. Davison/Davison and*
   Wood Ltd (f.e.1925) **See pages 7, 29, 38**
Brunswick (27 Old Durham Rd) *f.e.1833* **See pages 15, 28**
Buck see **Beaconsfield**
Burton House (BH) (197 Bensham Rd) *f.e.1886** **See pages 22, 26**
Bush (28 Oakwellgate) *f.e.1847 l.e.1918* **See page 8**
Butchers' Arms (BH) (257 High St/Park La) *f.e.1894** **See pages 13, 15**

Castle (137 Bensham Rd/Castle Pl) *f.e.1850 J. Reid/J. Reid and Sons Ltd (f.e.1899)* **See page 22**
Causeway/Causeway House/Causey House (35 Blue Quarries Rd) *f.e.1844 I. Tucker and Co Ltd (f.e.1939)*
   See pages 30, 40
Central (Half Moon La/Hills St) *f.e.1893 Swinburne and Co (f.e.1893) Newcastle Breweries Ltd (f.e.1933)*
   See pages 10, 43
Clavering Arms (15a Mulgrave Tce/Victoria St) *f.e.1858 l.e. 1933 I. Tucker and Co Ltd (f.e.1929)*
   See pages 18, 36, 38
Claxton (353 Sunderland Rd/Frank St) *f.e.1899 Newcastle Breweries Ltd (f.e.1933)* **See pages 26, 27, 40**
Coach and Horses (76 High St) *f.e.1844 I. Tucker and Co Ltd (f.e.1933)* **See pages 4, 11, 12**
Coach and Horses (High St, Wrekenton) *f.e.1851 R. Deuchar Ltd (f.e.1939)* **See pages 4, 30, 38**
Cock and Anchor (4 Cannon St) *f.e.1782 l.e.1913*
Commercial (Half Moon La/Hudson St) *f.e.1850 I. Tucker and Co Ltd (f.e.1909)* **See page 10**
Crawshay (BH) (also listed as **Crayshay**) (22 East St/Raglan Tce) *f.e.1869** **See pages 16, 17, 38, 48**
Crichton Arms/Crighton Arms (BH) (27 Prince Consort Rd) *f.e.1894**
Cricketers' Arms (39 Prince Consort Rd/Edward St) *f.e.1869 l.e. 1929 H. Fail and Co (f.e.1905) J. Rowell and*
   Son Ltd (f.e.1925)
Cromwell (38 Cromwell St, Mount Pleasant) *f.e.1869 I. Tucker and Co Ltd (f.e.1933)* **See pages 28, 29**
Cross House (12 Cross St, Mount Pleasant) *f.e.1879 (1865 as* **Crown***) Davison and Wood Ltd (f.e.1899)*
   See pages 7, 28, 38
Crown (137 High St) *f.e.1865 J. Rowell and Son Ltd (f.e.1929)* **See pages 12, 35, 42**
Crown (2 Coatsworth Rd/Bensham Rd) *f.e.1865 J. Deuchar Ltd (f.e.1905)* **See pages 22, 23, 35**
Crown (512 Durham Rd, Low Fell) *f.e.1847 R. Deuchar Ltd (f.e.1933)* **See pages 5, 32, 34, 37**
Crown and Thistle (89 Pipewellgate) *f.e.1790 l.e.1918* **See pages 8**
Crystal Palace (27 Oakwellgate/Garden St) *f.e.1858 (1833 as* **Royal Oak***) R. Deuchar Ltd (f.e1899)*
   See pages 16, 26, 40, 43
Curley's see **Phoenix**

Deckham (205 Old Durham Rd/Woods Tce) *f.e.1886 I. Tucker and Co Ltd (f.e.1899)* **See page 28**
Deptford House (Deptford Rd, Saltmeadows) *f.e.1850 l.e.1925* **See page 26**
Deptford see **New Deptford**
Dun Cow (65 High St) *f.e.1811 (1790 as* **Red Cow***) Swinburne and Co (f.e.1893 l.e.1913)*
   See pages 11, 12, 20, 37, 40

Eagle (7 Mulgrave Tce) *f.e.1869 l.e.1933 R. Deuchar Ltd (f.e1899 l.e.1933)* **See page 18**
Earl Grey (Stobbs Yd, Mirk La) *f.e.1869 l.e.1913*
Eglington Arms (BH) (4 Oakwellgate) *f.e.1869 l.e.1894**
Ellison Arms (164 High St/Ellison St) *f.e.1833 J. Rowell and Son Ltd (f.e.1933)* **See pages 17, 38, 39**
Ellison Arms (33 Park La/Trinity St) *f.e.1869 J. Deuchar Ltd (f.e.1899)* **See pages 17, 38, 39**
Eslington Arms see **Lord Eslington Arms**

Five Wand Mill/Ye Olde Five Wand Mille (203 Bensham Rd) *f.e.1833 A. Arrol and Sons Ltd (f.e.1913)*
   See pages 22, 36, 40
Flying Horse (31 Oakwellgate/Oakwellgate La) *f.e.1838 l.e.1918 Swinburne and Co (f.e.1899 l.e.1918)*
   See page 16
Foresters' Arms (BH) (413 Askew Road West/Derwentwater Rd) *f.e.1894** **See front cover, back cover and**
   pages 21, 34
Fountain (BH) (29 Peareth St) *f.e.1874 l.e.1894**
Fountain (10 Pipewellgate) *f.e.1782 l.e.1929 Wears and Watson (1909) J. Calder and Co (f.e.1913 l.e.1918)*
   See pages 6, 9
Fox and Lamb (1a Chandless St/Burdon St) *f.e.1869*
Full Moon/Half Moon (25 Bridge St) *f.e.1906 (1856 as Half Moon) l.e.1933 J. Deuchar Ltd (f.e.1929 l.e.1933)*
   See pages 4, 8, 23

Gardeners' Arms (271 Bensham Rd/Rawling Rd) *f.e.1865* **See page 23**
Gardeners' Arms/Free Gardeners' Arms (Carr Hill Rd) *f.e.1851 (1847/1874 as* **Oddfellows' Arms***)*
   See pages 29, 30
Gate (Salt Meadow Tce) *f.e.1874 l.e.1913*
Gateshead Arms (569 Durham Rd, Low Fell) *f.e.1847* **See pages 32, 33, 34**
George IV (708 Durham Rd, Low Fell) *f.e.1838 (probably 1828 as* **Sovereign***) Newcastle Breweries Ltd*
   (f.e.1933) **See pages 32, 33, 35, 38**
Glasgow House (BH) (259 Derwentwater Rd) *f.e.1874** **See page 21**
Globe (137 Old Durham Rd/Cross St) *f.e.1865 H. Fail and Co (f.e.1899) J. Rowell and Son Ltd (f.e.1925)*
   See pages 23, 28, 43
Globe (BH) (Pipewellgate) *f.e.1894** **See page 9**
Gloucester (BH) (31 High West St) *f.e.1874** **See pages 20, 25**
Goat (39 Bottle Bank) *f.e.1782 l.e.1925 Duncan and Co/Duncan and Daglish Ltd (f.e.1889 l.e.1925)*
   See pages 4, 9, 40

Golden Fleece/Old Golden Fleece (309 High St) *f.e.1865 J. Deuchar Ltd (f.e.1893) See pages 13, 14, 26, 43*
Grey Horse/Grey Horse Grill (99 High St) *f.e.1811 J.H. Graham/J.H. Graham Ltd (f.e.1889) Newcastle Hotels Ltd (f.e.1925) See pages 4, 11, 20*
Grey Nag's Head (219 High St/Oakwellgate Chare) *f.e.1869 J. Deuchar Ltd (f.e.1899) See pages 4, 12, 13, 36, 41, 43*

Half Moon (2 and 30 Half Moon La) *f.e.1828 (possibly 1811) Swinburne and Co (1893) Davison and Wood Ltd (f.e.1905) See pages 10, 35, 43*
Half Moon (Springwell Rd, Wrekenton) *f.e.1828 See pages 30, 31*
Half Moon (Bridge St) see **Full Moon**
Hawk (22 Bottle Bank) *f.e. 1811 l.e.1894 See page 4*
Hawks' Arms (also listed as Hawk's/Hawkes/Hawke's/Hawkes') (50 East St/St John's La) *f.e.1844 l.e.1918 See pages 16, 17, 38, 39*
Honeysuckle (92 Coatsworth Rd/Woodbine Tce) *f.e.1838 H. Fail and Co (f.e.1899) J. Rowell and Son Ltd (f.e.1925) See pages 7, 23, 38, 43*
Hutt's Arms (BH) (62 Park La/Burn St) *f.e.1886* See page 39*

Lambton Arms (BH) (listed as Lamton Arms) (128 High St) *f.e.1894**
Lime Kiln (South Shore Rd) *f.e.1850*
Lord Clyde (BH) (21 East St) *f.e. 1894**
Lord Eslington Arms/Eslington Arms (Eslington Rd) *f.e.1886 See pages 21, 23*
Lord Nelson (BH) (39 Nelson St/Lambton St) *f.e.1874 (possibly 1811)* See pages 18, 38*
Lord Raglan (BH) (137 High St) *f.e.1874 l.e.1894* See page 12*

Magpie (337 Derwentwater Rd/Atkinson Tce) *f.e.1844 Swinburne and Co (f.e.1905) Newcastle Breweries Ltd (f.e.1933) See pages 7, 21, 22, 40*
Masons' Arms (5 Jackson St) *f.e.1833 l.e.1893*
Masons' Arms (BH) (101 Burdon St) *f.e.1894* See page 5*
Metropole (246 High St/Jackson St) *f.e.1899 Swinburne and Co (f.e.1899) Newcastle Breweries Ltd (f.e.1933) See pages 13, 35, 36*
Moulders' Arms (24 Oakwellgate) *f.e.1847 l.e.1906*

Nelson (BH) (Nelson St) *f.e.1894**
Neptune (South Shore) *f.e.1844 l.e.1899*
Neville (123 High West St/Berwick St) *f.e.1869 H. Fail and Co (f.e.1899) J. Rowell and Son Ltd (f.e.1925) See pages 19, 20, 39, 43*
New Bridge (2 Bridge St) *f.e.1869 l.e.1918 See page 8*
New Deptford/Deptford (Deptford Rd, Saltmeadows) *f.e.1874 See page 26*
New Cannon (435 Durham Rd/Beacosfield Rd, Low Fell) *f.e.1828 See pages 4, 32, 33, 35, 36*
New Gateshead (Hawks St) *f.e.1869 See pages 5, 27, 36*
Northumberland Arms (BH) (55 Chandless St/Abbot St) *f.e.1874* See page 34*
Nursery House (BH) (11 Berwick St) *f.e.1894**

Old Cannon/Cannon (6 Cannon Row (Old Durham Rd)) *f.e.1828 See pages 30, 38, 39*
Old Fleece/Fleece/Ye Olde Fleece (289 High St/Chandless St) *f.e.1869 Wears and Watson Ltd (1929) J.G. Radcliffe Ltd (1933) A. Arrol and Sons Ltd (1939) See pages 14, 34*
Old Mill (113 West St/Jackson St) *f.e.1865 l.e.1933 S. Allsopp and Sons Ltd (1899) R. Deuchar Ltd (f.e.1905 l.e.1933) See pages 19, 40*
Old Nag's Head/Nag's Head (59 High St) *f.e.1782 F. Deuchar (1889) R. Deuchar Ltd (f.e.1899) See pages 4, 11, 12, 43*

Park House (253 High St/Park La) *f.e.1865 W. Wears/Wears and Watson (f.e.1905) Truman, Hanbury, Buxton and Co Ltd (1939) See pages 14, 15*
Patent Hammer (Hawks Rd) *f.e.1874 See pages 6, 26, 38*
Peareth Arms (BH) (337 High St) *f.e.1874* See page 13, 14*
Phoenix (Curley's) (266 High St/Charles St) *f.e.1879 (1865 as **Gorilla**) Northern Wine and Spirit Co Ltd (1899) Steel, Coulson and Co (1905) See pages 14, 15, 35, 39*
Plough (14 East St/Plough Yd) *f.e.1833 l.e.1913 Robinson and Anderson (f.e.1909 l.e.1913) See pages 16, 43*
Plough/Speed the Plough (369 Old Durham Rd) *f.e.1844 See pages 6, 29, 40*
Prince Albert (2 Forster St/Prince Consort Rd) *f.e.1938 See page 20*
Prince Alfred (17 Prince Consort Rd/Princess St) *f.e.1869 R. Deuchar Ltd (f.e.1909) See page 20*
Prince Consort (25 Prince Consort Rd/Albert St) *f.e.1869 See pages 19, 20*
Prince of Wales (BH) (1 Hampden St/Romulus St) *f.e.1865* J. Chipchase and Co (f.e.1899 l.e.1925) J.G. Radcliffe Ltd (f.e.1929 l.e.1933) J. Aitchison and Co Ltd (f.e.1939) See pages 20, 23*
Prince of Wales (BH) (63 Chandless St/Burn St) *f.e.1894* See page 17*
Princess Alice (2 High St, Wrekenton) *f.e.1874 l.e.1929 See pages 30, 31, 34*
Princess of Wales (16 Ellison St West/Grosvenor St) *f.e.1869 J. Deuchar Ltd (f.e.1929) See page 18*

Queen's (29 St James Rd) *f.e.1879 Swinburne and Co (f.e.1909) Newcastle Breweries Ltd (f.e.1933) See pages 26, 43*
Queen's Arms (25 Bridge St) *f.e.1844 l.e.1925 See page 41*
Queen's Head (16 High St. Bar in Mirk La) *f.e.1856 (possibly 1811) Wears and Watson (f.e.1909 l.e.1918) J.G. Radcliffe (1933) Northumberland Hotels (f.e.1939) See pages 4, 9, 36, 43*
Queen's Head (66 Sodhouse Bank (Old Durham Rd)) *f.e.1828 (possibly 1811) See pages 2, 29, 36*

Ravensworth/Ravensworth Castle (BH) (259 Bensham Rd) *f.e.1858* See page 22, 23*
Rector House (BH) (293 High St/Chandless St) *f.e.1894* See pages 13, 14, 34*
Redheugh (4 Askew Road West/Redheugh Bridge Rd) *f.e.1879 J. Mackay/Mackay and Co Ltd (f.e.1889) See page 21*
Richard Cobden (40 Chandless St/Park St) *f.e.1869 Swinburne and Co (f.e.1899) Newcastle Breweries Ltd (f.e.1933) See pages 16, 38*

Ridley Arms (BH) (13 Riddell St/Trinity St) *f.e.1874* See page 39*

Robin Hood (33 Church Wk) *f.e.1856 (possibly 1790) l.e.1913 See pages 8*

Rolling Mill Arms (BH) (2 Riddell St) *f.e.1894**

Royal (100 Prince Consort Rd/Chichester St) *f.e.1874 Swinburne and Co (f.e.1889) Newcastle Breweries Ltd (f.e.1933) See pages 20, 35, 43*

Royal Albert (BH) (48 Chandless St/Abbot St) *f.e.1886 l.e.1894* See page 20*

Royal Oak (High St, Wrekenton) *f.e.1828 (probably also* **Oak Tree***) See pages 30, 31*

Salt Meadows House/Saltmeadow (49 Salt Meadows Tce) *f.e.1874 A. Arrol and Sons Ltd (f.e.1939) See page 26*

Schooner see **Ship**

Scotch Arms (BH) (16 Cumberland St) *f.e.1886 l.e.1894**

Seven Stars (27 High St, Wrekenton) *f.e.1828 Newcastle Breweries Ltd (f.e.1929) See pages 7, 30, 31, 35*

Shakespeare (BH) (90 Fife St, Mount Pleasant) *f.e.1894* See pages 28, 29*

Ship (169 High St) *f.e.1858 (possibly 1847) J.G. Radcliffe (f.e.1925) Northumberland Hotels Ltd (f.e.1939) See page 13*

Ship (Wrekenton Row) *f.e.1828 (f.e.1925) I. Tucker and Co (f.e.1905) (Possibly also J.G. Radcliffe 1925/29 but may be printing error) See pages 4, 31*

Ship (Saltmeadows) *f.e.(possibly)1782 l.e.1925 ('Ship' entries for South Shore area confused)*

Ship (currently **Schooner**) (Tyne Main) *f.e.(possibly)1782 (1850 as Tyne Main) l.e.1925 See pages 27, 38*

Shipcote (32 Sunderland Rd/Sunderland St) *f.e.1865 J. Chipchase and Co (f.e.1893 l.e.1925) See pages 17*

Springfield (Durham Rd/Dryden Rd) *f.e.1939 Ind, Coope and Allsopp Ltd (f.e.1939) See pages 19, 22*

Springwell (Springwell Rd, Wrekenton) *f.e.1838 See page 31*

Stag (11 High St) *f.e.1899 l.e.1906*

Star (Hotel) (32 High West St/Edward St) *f.e.1869 R. Deuchar Ltd (f.e.1905) See pages 20, 35*

Star (Inn) (BH) (Forster St) *f.e.1894**

Station (6 Hills St) *f.e.1869 (1856 possibly 1851 as* **Railway/Railway Station***) Swinburne and Co (f.e.1905) Newcastle Breweries Ltd (f.e.1933) See back cover and pages 5, 10, 38*

Steamboat/Steam Boat/Steam Packet (5 Church St) *f.e.1833 l.e.1918 See pages 1, 6, 8, 38*

Swan (29 Swan St) *f.e.1844 l.e.1913 (White and Co. f.e.1909 l.e.1913) See page 16*

Swan see also **White Swan**

Talbot (BH) (61 West St/King William St) *f.e.1874* See page 19*

Three Tuns (88 Sodhouse Bank (Old Durham Rd)) *f.e.1828 Newcastle Breweries Ltd (f.e.1933) See pages 4, 7, 29, 30, 31, 37*

Travellers' Rest (1 Southend Tce (Old Durham Rd)) *f.e.1938 See pages 4, 23, 29, 38*

Turk's Head (68 High St) *f.e.1844 I. Tucker and Co/T.T. Tucker (f.e.1905) See pages 9, 11, 41*

Victoria (6 Coatsworth Rd/Romulus St) *f.e.1865 A. Deuchar Ltd (f.e.1899) See page 23*

Victoria (119 St Cuthberts Rd/Frederick St) *f.e.1879 (1869 as* **Underhand***) A. Arrol and Sons Ltd (f.e. 1899 l.e.1913) See page 42*

Victoria (Kells La, Low Fell) *f.e.1851 (possibly 1847 as* **Queen Adelaide***) See pages 5, 32, 34*

Vulcan (2 Quarry Field Rd) *f.e.1847 J. Rowell and Son Ltd (f.e.1933) See pages 26, 38*

Waggon (214 High Street/Wagon Yd (mis-spelt on map?)) *f.e.1811 l.e.1933 See pages 13, 15, 37*

Waggon Team (Lobley Hill Road) *f.e.1939 Newcastle Breweries Ltd (f.e.1939) See pages 7, 23*

Wheat Sheaf (13 High St) *f.e.1828 l.e.1906*

Whickham House (273 Bensham Rd/Rawling Rd) *f.e.1894* See page 23*

White Swan/Swan (8 Windy Nook Rd, Sheriff Hill) *f.e.1844 (intermittent entries) See pages 17, 23, 29, 30*

William IV (10 High St) *f.e.1838 (possibly 1833) Robinson and Anderson Ltd (f.e.1905) See page 43*

William IV (288 High St/Grahamsley St) *f.e.1838 (possibly 1833) Gibson and Co (1893) Swinburne and Co (f.e.1899 l.e.1909) Newcastle Breweries Ltd (f.e.1933) See pages 14, 15, 35*

Windmill (39 Charles St) *f.e.1847 l.e.1909 See page 40*

Wylam (BH) (10 Wylam St/Hector St) *f.e.1894* See pages 20*

Short index of Gateshead brewers, owners, early inns and newer pubs

New Pubs for Old – a list of the main post-war pubs

Azure Blue (Eastbourne Avenue), **Barley Mow** † (East Street), **Beacon** † (Beacon Lough), **Bensham Arms** † (Claremont Street), **British Queen** † (Split Crow Road), **Dun Cow** † (High Street), **Elephant on the Tyne** (Friars' Goose), **Foresters' Arms** † (Lower Teams), **Gloucester** (High West Street), **Gold Medal/Porcupine Park** (Chowdene Bank), **Greenmarket Inn** (TVTE), **Grove/Dinnings** † (High Street), **Lindisfarne/Grey Horse** † (Lindisfarne Drive), **Mitre** † (St Cuthbert's Village), **Park View/Ninepins** (Saltwell Road South), **Norwood** (Lobley Hill), **O'Keefe's** (High Street), **Old Fold Tavern** † (Park Lane), **Park Lane** † ('Civic Restaurant') (Park Lane), **Raven/Magpie** † (Beacon Lough East), **Ravensdene Lodge** (Lobley Hill), **Shakespeare Arms** (Mount Pleasant), **Stone Trough/Jolly Miller** (Chowdene), **Three Feathers** (Lyndhurst Estate, Low Fell), **Tilley Stone** (Jackson Street), **Trafalgar** † (Trinity Square), **Valley Farm** (TVTE), **Wrekendike** † (Wrekenton) († no longer trading as a pub)

Acknowledgements

Thanks to all those who have helped with the publication of this book either by encouragement, contributing material or helping check text. Thank-you Val and Tot Anderson; Peter Annable; Andrew Clark; Bob Dixon; Phil, George and Andy Dixon; John Donnelly; Gateshead Library staff; Yvonne Kennedy and family; Anthea Lang; Les May; Jackie Robinson; Joyce Robson; not forgetting Chris Boothroyd (a pubs widow, but not in the usual sense!). Image credits are due to Gateshead Libraries, Gateshead Local History Society and Trevor Ermel.

Some useful pub information sources

Frank Manders – *History of Gateshead* (Gateshead Corporation, 1973)

Lynn Pearson – *The Northumbrian Pub* (Sandhill Press, 1989)

Robert Colls and Bill Lancaster – *Newcastle upon Tyne: a modern history, Chapter 4 'Drinking in Newcastle'* by Brian Bennison (Phillimore, 2001)

Paul Jennings – *The Local: a history of the English pub* (Tempus, 2007)

Gateshead Libraries – collection of local Trade Directories relating to Gateshead

Gateshead Libraries – General index of newspaper and other useful articles

Gateshead Libraries – image collection (especially 'iSee Gateshead')

Gateshead Libraries – map collection, in particular OS 1:500 scale, 1898 edition

Tyne and Wear Archive Service – Building Control indexes and plans relating to Gateshead

Tyne and Wear Archive Service – Ale-house and Beer-house registers relating to Gateshead

'The Internet' – useful but beware recycled hearsay and unchecked research – so treat with caution!

Older residents – temporary guardians of invaluable and irreplaceable knowledge – but not always reliable!

The Crawshay in 1963.

Also available from Summerhill Books

Low Fell in Old Picture Postcards by Anthea Lang

Saltwell Park – The story of the 'People's Park' by Anthea Lang

Greenside Remembered by Mike Ingoe

visit our website to view our full range of books: **www.summerhillbooks.co.uk**